Reading & Writing
Machu Picchu

NATIONAL
GEOGRAPHIC
L E A R N I N G

Australia • Brazil • Mexico • Singapore • United Kingdom • United States

National Geographic Learning,
a Cengage Company

Reading & Writing, Machu Picchu

Laurie Blass, Mari Vargo, Keith S. Folse

Publisher: Sherrise Roehr

Executive Editor: Laura LeDréan

Managing Editor: Jennifer Monaghan

Digital Implementation Manager,
Irene Boixareu

Senior Media Researcher: Leila Hishmeh

Director of Global Marketing: Ian Martin

Regional Sales and National Account
Manager: Andrew O'Shea

Content Project Manager: Ruth Moore

Senior Designer: Lisa Trager

Manufacturing Planner: Mary Beth
Hennebury

Composition: Lumina Datamatics

For permission to use material from this text or product,
submit all requests online at **cengage.com/permissions**
Further permissions questions can be emailed to
permissionrequest@cengage.com

Student Edition: Reading & Writing, Machu Picchu
ISBN-13: 978-0-357-13825-0

National Geographic Learning
20 Channel Center Street
Boston, MA 02210
USA

Locate your local office at **international.cengage.com/region**

Visit National Geographic Learning online at **ELTNGL.com**
Visit our corporate website at **www.cengage.com**

Printed in China
Print Number: 02   Print Year: 2019

PHOTO CREDITS

Scope and Sequence

OUR WORLD 1

A busy street in central Bangkok, Thailand

ACADEMIC SKILLS

READING Scanning
WRITING / GRAMMAR Understanding sentence structure
Using simple present tense

THINK AND DISCUSS

1 How many people do you think are in the world today?
2 Which countries have the most people?

A **Look at the information on these pages and answer the questions.**

1. What is a megacity?
2. Which is the closest megacity to you?

B **Use the correct form of the words in blue to complete the sentences.**

Our _____ is the Earth and all the people and things on it.

A _____ is a place like Brazil, Spain, and Japan.

A _____ is a place like Tokyo, New York, and London.

10
New York-Newark, U.S.A.
18.6 million

7
Mexico City, Mexico
21.2 million

Los Angeles-
Long Beach-
Santa Ana, U.S.A.
12.3 million

5
São Paulo, Brazil
21.3 million

Lima, Peru
10.1 million

Rio de Janeiro,
Brazil
13.0 million

Buenos Aires,
Argentina
15.3 million

RISE OF THE MEGACITIES

As the world's population grows, more and more people are living in cities. Many of these people live in megacities—cities with populations of more than ten million. In 1951, there was just one megacity: New York. In 2016, there were 31 megacities in countries all around the world.

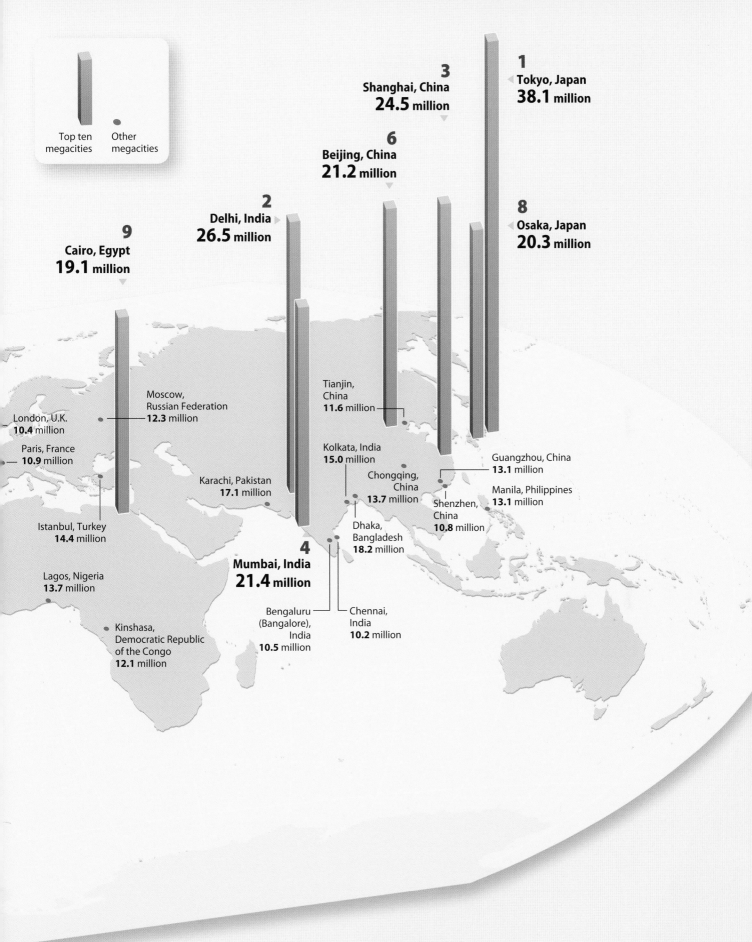

3
Shanghai, China
24.5 million

1
Tokyo, Japan
38.1 million

6
Beijing, China
21.2 million

2
Delhi, India
26.5 million

8
Osaka, Japan
20.3 million

9
Cairo, Egypt
19.1 million

Top ten megacities

Other megacities

Moscow, Russian Federation
12.3 million

London, U.K.
10.4 million

Paris, France
10.9 million

Karachi, Pakistan
17.1 million

Tianjin, China
11.6 million

Kolkata, India
15.0 million

Chongqing, China
13.7 million

Guangzhou, China
13.1 million

Manila, Philippines
13.1 million

Shenzhen, China
10.8 million

Istanbul, Turkey
14.4 million

Dhaka, Bangladesh
18.2 million

Lagos, Nigeria
13.7 million

4
Mumbai, India
21.4 million

Kinshasa, Democratic Republic of the Congo
12.1 million

Bengaluru (Bangalore), India
10.5 million

Chennai, India
10.2 million

Source: The World's Cities in 2016, United Nations

Reading 1 QUICK READ SEE PAGE 110

PREPARING TO READ

BUILDING
VOCABULARY

A The words in blue below are used in the reading passage on pages 5–6. Match the sentence parts to make definitions. Use a dictionary to help you.

1. A **restaurant** _____   a. is a place where people stay for a short time.

2. A **job** _____   b. is a place where you buy and eat food.

3. A **hotel** _____   c. is a place away from cities and towns.

4. The **countryside** _____   d. is the work you do to make money.

BUILDING
VOCABULARY

B Read the definitions. Use the correct form of the words in blue to complete the sentences (1–3).

> If something is **large**, it is big.
> If something **grows**, it becomes bigger.
> If two people or things are **different**, they are not the same.

1. Australia is a very _____ country, but fewer than 25 million people live there.

2. Cities around the world are continuing to _____. There are now 31 cities with a population of over ten million.

3. Shenzhen, China, has changed a lot in the last 50 years. Life there is now very _____ from before.

USING
VOCABULARY

C List three ideas for each category below. Then share your ideas with a partner.

1. three **cities** you like

   _____   _____   _____

2. three **large** countries

   _____   _____   _____

3. three things you can see in the **countryside**

   _____   _____   _____

PREDICTING

D Look up the word *typical* in your dictionary. Then read the title and look at the photos on pages 5 and 6. What do you think the reading is mainly about? Check your prediction as you read the passage.

1. a typical person
2. a typical day on Earth
3. life in a typical city

THE FACE OF SEVEN BILLION

Track 1

A In a world of more than seven billion people, is there a "most typical" person? According to statistics, there is. He's a 28-year-old Han Chinese man. He lives in a city, can read and write, and probably works in a hotel or restaurant.

B There are 1.01 men in the world for every woman, so the typical person is male. China, with over 1.3 billion people, is the country with the largest population. The largest ethnic group[1] is Han Chinese, and the world's largest age group is 28.

[1]An **ethnic group** is a group of people from one race or culture.

C More people—51 percent of the world's population—live in a city than in the countryside. The most common[2] job is in services, such as restaurant and hotel work. Eighty-two percent of the world's population can read and write.

D What does the typical person look like? Look at the two faces on this page. The pictures were made by researchers at the Chinese Academy of Sciences. They used thousands of photos of 28-year-old Han Chinese men and women. They used them to make images of the typical man and woman on Earth today.

E What will the typical person be like in the future? The world's population is growing and changing all the time. Every second, five people are born and two people die. In 1800, there were 1 billion people on Earth. Now, there are over 7 billion. By 2045, there may be 9 billion. So the typical person of the future may be very different from today.

[2]If something is **common**, it is found in large numbers or happens often.

▼ **Researchers in Beijing created these images of the typical woman and man in the world today.**

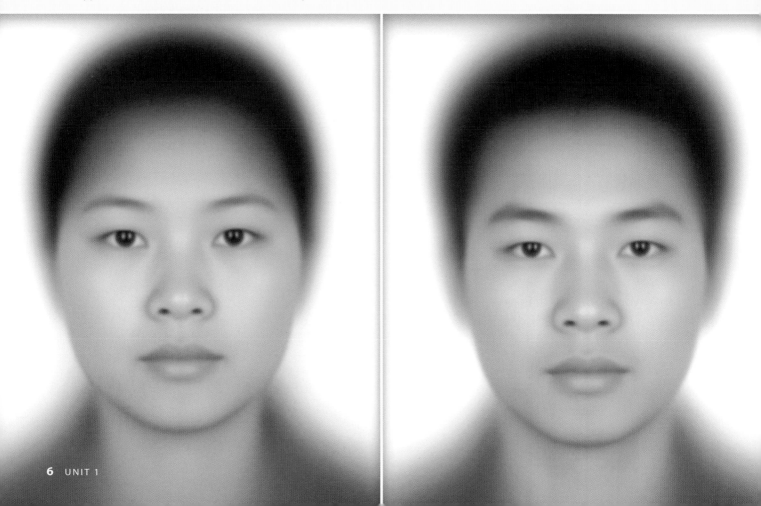

UNDERSTANDING THE READING

A Complete the chart with information about the typical person.

	Typical person
1. Lives in a city or the countryside?	
2. Job?	
3. Age?	
4. Male or female?	
5. Country and ethnic group?	

B Complete each sentence (1–5) with the correct numbers from the reading.

1. About _____ percent of people live in a city.

2. For every woman on Earth, there are _____ men.

3. The population of China is about _____ .

4. The most common age of people living today is _____ .

5. _____ percent of people can read and write.

C Find and underline the following words in the reading. Use the context—the words around the word—to help you understand its meaning. Then match the words to the correct definitions.

> **statistics** (paragraph A)   **researchers** (paragraph D)   **images** (paragraph D)

1. A **statistic** _____   a. is a photo or picture.
2. A **researcher** _____   b. is a number used to give information.
3. An **image** _____   c. is a person who finds information about something.

> **CRITICAL THINKING**   When you **reflect** on ideas and information, you connect them with your own experience. Ask yourself these questions as you read: *What do I think about this? How does this relate to my life?*

D Look back at the chart in **A**. Note your answers to the same questions below. How similar are you to the "typical person" described in the passage? Discuss with a partner.

1. _____   2. _____   3. _____
4. _____   5. _____

DEVELOPING READING SKILLS

> **READING SKILL** Scanning
>
> Scanning helps you find important, or *key*, details quickly. When you scan, you move your eyes quickly over the text and look for specific things. For example, you can look for **numbers** to find times, dates, amounts, ages, and distances. You can also look for **number words** such as *one, two, three, hundred, thousand, million, billion,* and *percent*.

SCANNING **A** Scan the following paragraph and circle all the numbers.

At the moment, China is the country with the largest population. However, many people think that this will change by 2030. India's population is expected to grow to around 1.5 billion by that time, making it the largest in the world. China's population will also grow, but only to around 1.4 billion. The United States will stay as the third largest country, and Indonesia will stay as fourth. In 2015, Brazil had the fifth largest population. But by 2030, it is expected that Nigeria's population will grow to just over 260 million. That will make Nigeria the fifth largest country in the world by population.

SCANNING **B** Now complete the chart using the information in the paragraph above.

Largest countries by population in 2015	Largest countries by predicted population in 2030
1. China (1.38 billion)	1. _____ (1.53 billion)
2. India (1.31 billion)	2. _____ (1.42 billion)
3. United States (322 million)	3. _____ (356 million)
4. Indonesia (258 million)	4. _____ (295 million)
5. Brazil (208 million)	5. _____ (262 million)

SCANNING **C** Scan paragraph E on page 6 and answer the questions.

1. How many people were on the planet in 1800? _____

2. How many people are there now? _____

3. How many people might there be in 2045? _____

4. How many people are born every second? How many people die? _____

Video

Spain and Portugal as viewed from the International Space Station

7 BILLION

BEFORE VIEWING

A What is the population of your country? Is it going up or down? Discuss with a partner.   DISCUSSION

B Look at the information below about the world's population. Then answer the questions.   LEARNING ABOUT THE TOPIC

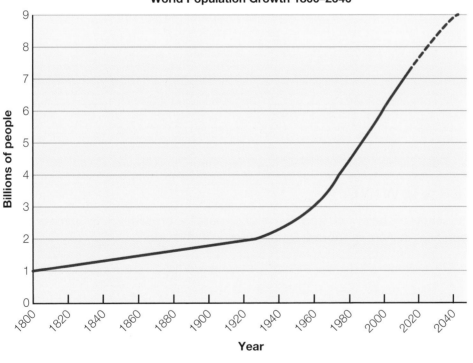

World Population Growth 1800–2040

1. When did the world's population start to grow more quickly?

_____

2. Why do you think this happened?

_____

C The words in **bold** below are used in the video. Match each word with the correct definition.

> People in rich countries **consume** most of the world's meat.
> The **average** person born in 2015 will live for 75 years.
> If the population grows too much, some people may not have **adequate** food and water.
> In the future, we will need to use more wind, water, and solar **energy**.

1. _____ (adj) usual, typical, or normal

2. _____ (adj) enough

3. _____ (v) to use, eat, or drink something

4. _____ (n) the power that makes things work

WHILE VIEWING

UNDERSTANDING MAIN IDEAS

A ▶ Watch the video. Check (✓) the topics you learn about.

☐ 1. the speed at which the world population is growing

☐ 2. the movement of people from the countryside to the city

☐ 3. the countries that are growing the fastest

☐ 4. differences between rich and poor people in the world

UNDERSTANDING DETAILS

B ▶ Watch the video a second time and complete the sentences.

1. In 2010, the average person lived for _____ years. In 1960, the average person lived for _____ years.

2. In 1975, there were _____ megacities. Now there are _____.

3. Five percent of the population uses 23 percent of the world's _____.

4. Thirteen percent of people don't have _____.

AFTER VIEWING

CRITICAL THINKING: SYNTHESIZING

A The sentences below are from the reading passage on pages 5–6. Check (✓) the sentences that are supported by information in the video.

☐ 1. There are 1.01 men in the world for every woman.

☐ 2. More people … live in a city than in the countryside.

☐ 3. Eighty-two percent of the world's population can read and write.

☐ 4. Every second, five people are born and two people die.

☐ 5. In 1800, there were 1 billion people on Earth.

Reading 2 QUICK READ SEE PAGE 113

PREPARING TO READ

A The words in **blue** below are used in the reading passage on pages 12–13. Complete the definitions using the correct form of the words.

BUILDING VOCABULARY

With **around** 100 million users, LinkedIn is a very **popular** social networking **site**. **However**, it's very different from sites like Facebook. LinkedIn is used mostly by working people. Users **visit** the site to **add** information about their careers and connect with people who have similar jobs. The site also gives **news** about **available** jobs that users might be interested in.

1. If you _____ to something, you make a group of things bigger.

2. If you say a number is _____ one million, it is not exactly one million, but very close.

3. If something is _____ , you can get it or use it.

4. _____ means the same as *but* or *on the other hand*.

5. _____ is information you didn't know before.

6. If something is _____ , many people like it.

7. A _____ is a place on the Internet.

8. If you _____ a place or website, you go there.

B Note answers to the questions below. Then discuss with a partner.

USING VOCABULARY

1. What are the most **popular** social media **sites** in your country?

   _____

2. Do you often read **news** online? Which websites do you use?

   _____

3. Which websites can you **visit** to find out about **available** jobs in your country?

   _____

C Work with a partner. Guess the answers to the questions below. Then scan the reading passage to check your guesses.

PREDICTING

1. What percentage of the world's population uses social media regularly?

   _____

2. How much time does an average person spend on social media each day?

   _____

A CONNECTED WORLD

🎧 Track 2

A Do you know what your friends watched on TV last night? Do your friends know what you had for breakfast today? Do you think you're using social media too much?

B Social media is now a part of many people's everyday lives. Estimates[1] suggest that around 2.8 billion people use social media regularly. That's almost 40 percent of the world's population. But how much time do we really spend on social media? And what exactly do we spend that time doing?

C Research shows that, worldwide, the average person spends two hours and 19 minutes on social media each day. People in the Philippines are the most active users. An average person there spends four hours and 17 minutes a day on social media. Research also suggests that women use social media more than men. In the United States, for example, women spend around two hours more per week than men on social media.

D What do most people do on social media? In general, it seems we spend more time looking at other people's pages than adding to our own. According to one survey, the most common social media activities are visiting friends' pages, reading their news, and commenting on their posts.

E The most popular social media site is Facebook, with over 2 billion users. In second place, however, is the Chinese site Qzone. In 2017, Qzone was China's most popular social media site, with around 600 million users worldwide. That's more than Twitter and Instagram.

F Social media continues to grow. Right now, there are five new Facebook profiles every second. And as Internet access[2] becomes available to even more people around the world, this growth won't stop anytime soon.

[1]An estimate is a good guess based on facts.
[2]If someone has Internet access, they are able to connect to the Internet.

The world's most active social media users
(average time spent on social media per day)

Most popular social media sites
(based on the number of users in 2017)

Most common social media activities
(based on 2016 Nielsen Social Media Report)

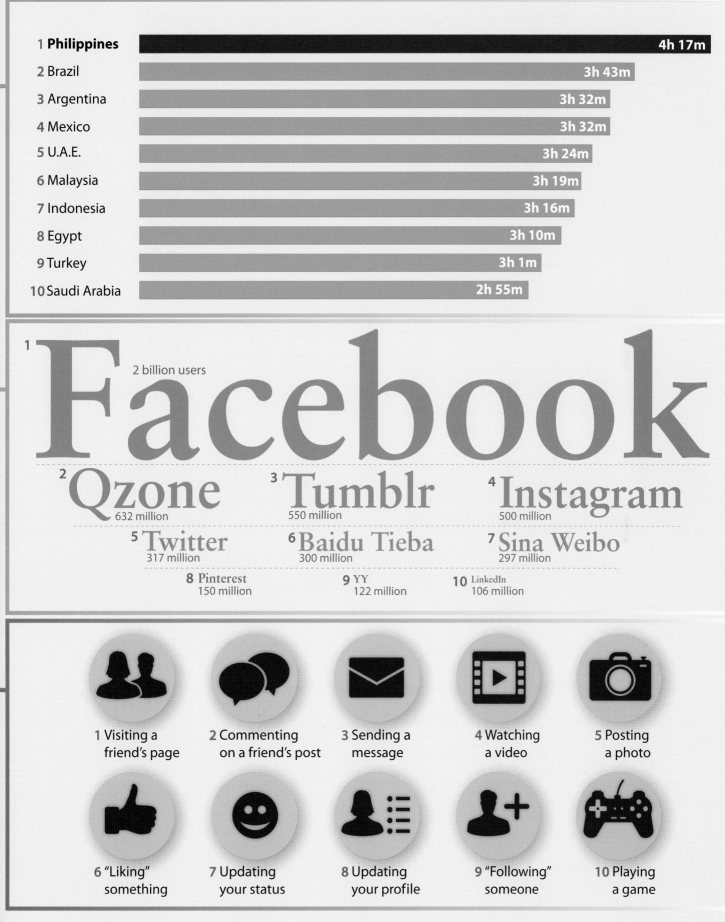

1	**Philippines**	4h 17m
2	Brazil	3h 43m
3	Argentina	3h 32m
4	Mexico	3h 32m
5	U.A.E.	3h 24m
6	Malaysia	3h 19m
7	Indonesia	3h 16m
8	Egypt	3h 10m
9	Turkey	3h 1m
10	Saudi Arabia	2h 55m

1 Facebook
2 billion users

2 Qzone
632 million

3 Tumblr
550 million

4 Instagram
500 million

5 Twitter
317 million

6 Baidu Tieba
300 million

7 Sina Weibo
297 million

8 Pinterest
150 million

9 YY
122 million

10 LinkedIn
106 million

1 Visiting a friend's page

2 Commenting on a friend's post

3 Sending a message

4 Watching a video

5 Posting a photo

6 "Liking" something

7 Updating your status

8 Updating your profile

9 "Following" someone

10 Playing a game

UNDERSTANDING THE READING

UNDERSTANDING MAIN IDEAS

A Match each of these main ideas with a paragraph (A–F) from the reading.

_____ 1. Facebook and Qzone are popular social media sites.

_____ 2. The amount of time people spend on social media varies by country and by gender.

_____ 3. On social media, people spend most of their time on friends' pages.

_____ 4. Many people around the world use social media regularly.

INTERPRETING VISUAL DATA

B Use the reading passage and infographic on pages 12–13 to answer the questions.

1. Which social media sites have 500 million users or more?

_____

2. In how many countries does the average user spend more than three hours a day on social media?

_____

3. How many more users did Facebook have than Twitter in 2017?

_____

4. On social media, is it more common for someone to post a photo or look at a friend's photo?

_____

CRITICAL THINKING: GUESSING MEANING FROM CONTEXT

C Find and underline the following words in the reading on pages 12–13. Use the context—the words around the word—to help you understand their meanings. Complete the definitions.

regularly (paragraph B) **active** (paragraph C) **survey** (paragraph D)

1. If someone is _____, they are always doing things.

2. If you do a _____, you find out information by asking people questions.

3. If you do something _____, you do it often.

CRITICAL THINKING: PERSONALIZING

D Discuss your answers to these questions with a partner.

1. How much time do you spend on social media?

_____

2. What do you usually do on social media?

_____

3. Are your habits similar to or different from the ones in the infographic on pages 12–13?

_____

Writing

EXPLORING WRITTEN ENGLISH

A Read the information below.

LANGUAGE FOR WRITING What is a Sentence?

A **sentence** is a group of words that expresses an idea. Most types of sentences have at least one subject and one verb. It should begin with a **capital letter** and should end with a **punctuation** mark, such as a period (.), question mark (?), or exclamation point (!).

subject   verb

He   lives   in a city.

capital letter   punctuation

If a sentence does not have a subject and a verb, it is a **fragment**. Here are two examples. What is missing in each one?

Created a picture of the typical man and woman.
The 28-year-old age group the largest.

Now underline the subject and circle the verb in each sentence (1–5). (Two sentences have more than one subject and verb.)

1. I use my phone every day.
2. My brother and I don't call each other very often.
3. Every day, my friends send me emails or texts.
4. He always goes online when he's watching TV.
5. I connect on my phone when I don't have my laptop.

A young woman checks her cell phone at the Waterfront Promenade in Hong Kong.

B Read the items below (1–7). Check (✓) each complete sentence. If it is a fragment, what is missing? Write **S** for *subject* or **V** for *verb*.

☐ 1. The "most typical" person from China. _____

☐ 2. The population bigger every year. _____

☐ 3. Cell phones are also known as mobile phones. _____

☐ 4. Researchers used thousands of photos of 28-year-old people. _____

☐ 5. Lives in a big city, not a small country town. _____

☐ 6. My school's library has 50 computers for students. _____

☐ 7. I never the computers in the library. _____

C Change the fragments in exercise B into complete sentences using your own ideas.

D Unscramble the words to make sentences. Then underline the subjects and circle the verbs.

1. cell phones / people / A lot of / have / .

   _____

2. goes / to the library / every day / My best friend / .

   _____

3. all over / Internet / the world / use the / People from / .

   _____

4. are / heavy / not very / Tablets / .

   _____

E Read the information below. Then complete each sentence (1–6 on page 17) with the correct form of *be*. Use the simple present tense.

> **LANGUAGE FOR WRITING** Simple Present Tense of *Be*
>
> We use the simple present for habits, daily routines, facts, or things that are generally true. The simple present tense of *be* has three forms: *am, is,* and *are.*
>
> | | |
> |---|---|
> | I | **am / 'm** |
> | he / she / it | **is / 's** |
> | you / we / they | **are / 're** |
>
> We usually use nouns, adjectives, or prepositional phrases after *be.*
>
> *I am a **student**.*   *I like Pinterest. It's **fun**.*   *The books are **on the desk**.*

1. My favorite social networking site _____ Tagged.

2. My brothers _____ in Seoul.

3. My sister _____ a doctor.

4. I think social media _____ a great way to meet people.

5. Facebook and Twitter _____ fun.

6. I _____ in law school.

F Read the information below.

LANGUAGE FOR WRITING Simple Present Tense of Other Verbs

For verbs other than *be*, use the base form with *I, you, we*, and *they*. For most verbs, use the base form + *-s* with *he, she*, and *it*.

> I **like** Pinterest.   She **likes** Pinterest. We **like** Pinterest.
> I **use** Twitter.   Mark (or He) **uses** Twitter. Kim and Leo (or They) **use** Twitter.

If a verb ends in *-y*, drop the *-y* and add *-ies*.

> I **study** at night.   Kay **studies** in the morning.   They **study** after lunch.

Some verbs do not follow the usual rule. You do not use the base form + *-s* with *he, she*, and *it*. Instead, these verbs have irregular forms.

> She **does** her homework on a tablet.
> Alex **goes** to school at 9:00 a.m.
> Tomas **has** a laptop, a tablet, and a smartphone.

Now complete each pair of sentences (1–5) with the correct form of a verb from the box. Use the simple present tense.

like	live	speak	study	use

1. I _____ science for about two hours every day.

   My sister _____ science for about three hours a day.

2. I _____ Twitter better than Facebook.

   Joe _____ Facebook better than Twitter.

3. Pam and Luke _____ in the country.

   Alex _____ in the city.

4. Tina _____ three languages: Spanish, French, and English.

   I _____ two languages: English and Mandarin.

5. Matt and Kim _____ the computers in the library.

   James _____ the computers in the coffee shop.

WRITING TASK

GOAL You are going to write sentences on the following topic:
Describe yourself and your communication habits.

PLANNING **A** Write answers to the questions (1–6). Write notes (not complete sentences). Then share your answers with a partner.

About yourself:

1. Where do you live? _____

2. What languages do you speak? _____

3. Do you have a job? If yes, what is it? If not, what do you want to do?

_____

About your communication habits:

4. How do you connect with friends online? _____

5. How long do you spend on social media in a typical day? _____

6. What websites do you like? _____

FIRST DRAFT **B** Use your notes to write four or more sentences about yourself and your communication habits. Use the simple present tense of *be* and other verbs in your sentences.

Example: I live in Tokyo, Japan.

EDITING **C** Now edit your draft. Correct mistakes with the simple present. Use the checklist on page 124.

UNIT REVIEW
Answer the following questions.

1. What is a megacity?

_____

_____

2. When do you use the simple present tense?

_____

_____

3. Do you remember the meanings of these words? Check (✔) the ones you know. Look back at the unit and review the ones you don't know.

Reading 1:

☐ city   ☐ country   ☐ countryside
☐ different   ☐ grow   ☐ hotel
☐ job [AWL]   ☐ large   ☐ restaurant
☐ world

Reading 2:

☐ add   ☐ around   ☐ available [AWL]
☐ however   ☐ news   ☐ popular
☐ site [AWL]   ☐ visit

NOTES

Verbs: Simple Present Tense

Three monks hold a lantern at the Yi Peng sky lantern festival in Chiang Mai, Thailand.

OBJECTIVES **Grammar:** To learn about simple present tense
Vocabulary and Spelling: To study common words with the sound of **i** in f**i**sh
Writing: To write about things that people usually do

Can you write about things that people usually do?

Grammar for Writing

I **wake up** early.

I **eat** bread and jam for breakfast.

I **go** (to school) by bus.

What Is a Verb?

✓ A **verb** is a word that shows action (or existence).

> I **teach** English every day.
>
> I **am** a teacher at Wilson College.
>
> I **drive** to school at 7:30 a.m.
>
> I **arrive** at school at 8:00 a.m.
>
> My first class **begins** at 8:30 a.m.
>
> It **is** a writing class.

✓ The tense of the verb usually tells the time of the action. (The Brief Writer's Handbook explains tenses.)

Simple Present Tense

✓ **Simple present tense** is used for actions that happen many times or are always true. (See Brief Writer's Handbook for other verb tenses.)

✓ Common time expressions for simple present tense include **always, never,** and **every.**

✓ In simple present tense, each verb has two forms: **live, lives.**

20 Common Verbs You Need to Know*	
1. **am**	I **am** from the United States.
2. **are**	Your answers **are** excellent.
3. **come**	We never **come** home late.
4. **find**	Can you **find** my country on that map?
5. **get**	I **get** many e-mails every day.

*Based on the General Service List, Corpus of Contemporary American English, and other corpus sources

6. give	The teacher **gives** a test to every student.
7. go	You **go** to school by car.
8. has	My name **has** ten letters.
9. have	We **have** many friends.
10. is	Everything **is** OK.
11. know	You **know** French and Spanish.
12. like	She **likes** coffee with milk and sugar.
13. look	Please **look** at question number ten.
14. make	I **make** coffee every morning.
15. say	Please **say** your name slowly.
16. see	I **see** you.
17. take	Please **take** a cookie.
18. think	I **think** the time is seven o'clock.
19. use	I **use** my cell phone many times every day.
20. work	He **works** at the bank.

ACTIVITY 1 **Finding Verbs in Sentences**

Circle the ten verbs in these sentences. Each sentence has one verb.

My Mondays

1. Monday (is) a difficult day for me.

2. My day begins very early.

3. I take a shower at 6 a.m.

4. I drink a cup of coffee with milk and sugar.

5. I eat a light breakfast.

6. I usually eat toast with jam.

7. Sometimes I eat cereal with milk.

8. Then I go to school.

9. I have five classes on Monday.

10. I am usually tired after school.

Writing Sentences about Actions

Read the sentences. Then fill in the missing verbs from the word bank. Write the sentences with a capital letter and a period.

make	eat	fly	run
swim	jump	are	sit

Talking about Animals

1. giraffes .... leaves

_____

2. penguins .... black and white

_____

3. fish .... in the ocean

_____

4. horses .... very fast

_____

5. monkeys .... in trees

_____

6. birds .... in the sky

_____

7. bees .... honey

_____

8. frogs .... over rocks and plants

_____

Two Verb Forms of Simple Present Tense: -s and no -s

✓ In simple present tense, verbs have two forms.

Simple Form*	speak, write, do	the verb as in the dictionary with no endings (no –s, no –ed, no –ing)
The –s or –es Form**	speak**s**, write**s**, do**es**	the verb + –s or –es

*base form or dictionary form
** 3rd person singular

✓ For verbs with **I, you, we,** and **they,** use the dictionary form.

✓ For verbs with **he, she,** and **it,** use the form that ends in –s.

	make	**know**	**think**
Singular	I **make** you **make** he **makes** she **makes** it **makes**	I **know** you **know** he **knows** she **knows** it **knows**	I **think** you **think** he **thinks** she **thinks** it **thinks**
Plural	we **make** you **make** they **make**	we **know** you **know** they **know**	we **think** you **think** they **think**

✓ For verbs that end in –o, –ch, –sh, –ss, and –x, add –es.

–o	**–ch**	**–sh**	**–ss**	**–x**
I **go** she **goes**	we **watch** he **watches**	you **wash** it **washes**	I **guess** he **guesses**	they **mix** she **mixes**

Spelling Verbs with –es

Write the correct form of the verb with each subject.

1. teach	**2.** finish	**3.** pass	**4.** do
you *teach*	he	I	it
she *teaches*	we	the bus	children

5. miss	**6.** catch	**7.** go	**8.** push
you	he	my plane	you
she	we	people	he

✓ English has 26 letters: 5 vowels (**a, e, i, o, u**) and 21 consonants.
   • For verbs that end in a consonant + **y**, change the –**y** to –**i** and add –**es**.
   • For verbs that end in a vowel + **y**, add –**s**.

consonant + y		vowel + y	
I **try**	they **cry**	I **say**	we **play**
she **tries**	the baby **cries**	he **says**	the boy **plays**

Spelling Verbs with –s or –ies

Write the correct form of the verb with each subject.

1. study	**2.** carry	**3.** buy	**4.** stay
we	she	they	we
she	you	the doctor	my uncle

5. hurry	**6.** try	**7.** fly	**8.** enjoy
you	a student	pilots	every child
she	students	a pilot	children

Irregular Verbs in Simple Present Tense

✓ The verbs **be** and **have** are irregular. You must memorize the forms of these verbs.

	be	have
singular	I **am** you **are** he **is** she **is** it **is**	I **have** you **have** he **has** she **has** it **has**
Plural	we **are** you **are** they **are**	we **have** you **have** they **have**

Common Student Mistakes

Student Mistake X	Problem	Correct Example ✓
Ed and **Linda in** Texas.	verb missing	Ed and Linda **live** in Texas.
Ed **work** in a big office.	**–s** ending missing	Ed work**s** in a big office.
Ed **is wakes up** at 6 a.m. every day.	extra verb	Ed **wakes up** at 6 a.m. every day.
Ed **trys** to sleep seven hours every night.	spelling of the verb	Ed tr**ies** to sleep seven hours every night.

ACTIVITY 5 **Writing Verbs in Sentences**

Read the sentences about one man's job. Then fill in the missing words from the word bank.

takes	eats	watches	is	takes
drives	puts	wakes	begins	listens

A Taxi Driver

1. Ahmed _____ a taxi driver.

2. He _____ a taxi from 8 a.m. to 4 p.m. five days a week.

3. He _____ up at 6:30 a.m.

4. He _____ his day with a cup of black coffee.

5. He _____ a quick shower.

6. Ahmed _____ on a pair of pants and a nice shirt.

27

7. Then he _____ something for breakfast.

8. Sometimes he _____ the morning news on TV.

9. Ahmed _____ to news on the radio in his taxi.

10. He _____ customers to many different places.

ACTIVITY 6 **Writing Complete Sentences**

Circle the verb in each sentence. Then copy the sentences. Use capital letters and periods.

My Class

1. i (study) english at smith college

   I study English at Smith College.
   _____

2. my english is not so good

   _____

3. i am in the beginning class

   _____

4. my class has 12 students

   _____

5. i am from saudi arabia

   _____

6. four students come from japan

   _____

7. they speak japanese

_____

8. five students speak spanish

_____

9. they come from mexico and peru

_____

10. meilin is from china

_____

11. she speaks chinese

_____

12. one student comes from korea

_____

13. his name is kwan

_____

14. i like all the students in my class very much

_____

Negative of Verbs in Simple Present Tense

Making a negative is very easy. You use a special helping verb—**do** or **does**—before the word **not**.

✓ Use **do not** + verb after **I, you, we** or **they**.

✓ Use **does not** + verb after **he, she,** or **it**.

	have	know	do
Singular	I **do not** have	I **do not** know	I **do not** do
	you **do not** have	you **do not** know	you **do not** do
	he **does not** have	he **does not** know	he **does not** do
	she **does not** have	she **does not** know	she **does not** do
	it **does not** have	it **does not** know	it **does not** do
Plural	we **do not** have	we **do not** know	we **do not** do
	you **do not** have	you **do not** know	you **do not** do
	they **do not** have	they **do not** know	they **do not** do

✓ You can also use a short form: **doesn't, don't**. This is called a **contraction**. It is used in speaking and in friendly writing such as e-mail. Do not use contractions in formal writing.

Full Form	I **do not** have a problem.	Use in academic writing
	He **does not** know the answer.	(or in very formal speaking).
	It **does not** make any difference.	
Contraction	I **don't** have a problem.	Use in e-mail and friendly writing
	He **doesn't** know the answer.	(or in conversation).
	It **doesn't** make any difference.	

Common Student Mistakes

Student Mistake X	Problem	Correct Example ✓
Ed and Linda **no live** in Korea.	wrong negative	Ed and Linda **do not live** in Korea.
Ed **do not works** in a big office.	–s ending on verb	Ed **does not work** in a big office.
Ed **is not** wake up at 7 a.m. every day.	wrong verb with **not**	Ed **does not** wake up at 7 a.m. every day.

ACTIVITY 7 **Writing Negative Sentences**

The information about these countries is not correct. Write the sentences again. Use negative verbs. Be careful with capital letters and periods.

Information about Seven Countries

1. people in brazil speak spanish

   People in Brazil do not speak Spanish.

2. the flag of colombia has four colors

3. most people in canada work on sunday

4. the capital of japan is kyoto

5. most people in saudi arabia work on friday

6. drivers in dubai drive on the left side of the street

7. the flag of the united states has five colors

_____

8. people in japan speak chinese

_____

ACTIVITY 8 **Scrambled Sentences**

Change the order of the words to write a correct sentence. Be careful with spelling, capital letters, punctuation, and word order.

Jason Thompson's Job

1. very jason a job thompson important has

_____

2. he of president a is the company

_____

3. he company every goes to his day

_____

4. to the company he seven gets at

_____

5. leaves at six he

_____

6. not go does home early he

_____

7. talks with many he people

_____

8. free he lot of does not have a time

_____

9. happy very he is his job at

_____

ACTIVITY 9 **Finding and Correcting 10 Mistakes**

Circle the ten mistakes. Then write the sentences correctly. The number in parentheses ( ) is the number of mistakes in that sentence. Be ready to explain your answers.

Our New Year's Celebration in Mexico

1. I am from mexico. (1)

_____

2. My favorit holiday is New Year's. (1)

_____

3. We celebrate it at Midnight on December 31. (1)

_____

4. We are eat 12 grapes in one minute. (1)

_____

5. We eat one grapes for each month of the year. (1)

_____

6. We make a wish for 12 good thing for the new year. (1)

_____

7. My famili and I eat a really big dinner together. (1)

_____

8. Sometimes we eat Turkey. (1)

_____

9. Sometimes we eats a special Mexican food called mole. (1)

_____

10. My family and I not leave our house on this important day. (1)

_____

Track 3 •))) **ACTIVITY 10** **Dictation**

You will hear six sentences three times. Listen carefully and write the six sentences. The number in parentheses ( ) is the number of words in the sentence. Be careful with capital letters and end punctuation.

1. _____ (7)

2. _____ (6)

3. _____ (8)

4. _____ (5)

5. _____ (6)

6. _____ (5)

ACTIVITY 11 **Practicing Grammar and Vocabulary in Model Writing**

Read the sentences in the paragraph very carefully. Fill in the missing words from the word bank. Circle the fourteen letters that need to be capital letters. Then copy the paragraph on your own paper.

| always | lincoln | call | play | and |
| breakfast | every | they | are | at |

Twin Sisters

1 laura _____ maria are students. 2 _____ like school very

much. 3 they go to _____ high school. 4 they eat breakfast _____

7:00 a.m. 5 they enjoy _____ very much. 6 they _____ eat eggs and

bread for breakfast. 7 sometimes they _____ their friends after breakfast. 8 they

_____ good students. 9 _____ night they study for an exam.

10 sometimes they _____ video games on the computer.

ACTIVITY 12 **Guided Writing: Making Changes in Model Writing**

Write the paragraph from Activity 11 again, but make the changes listed below. Sometimes you will have to make other changes, too.

Sentence 1. Change **Laura and Maria** to **Maria**. Then make changes in the other sentences. Be careful with subject–verb agreement.

Sentence 4. Change the time to any other reasonable time to eat breakfast.

Sentence 7. Change **call** to **text**.

Sentence 8. Change **good** to **excellent**.

Sentence 9. Change **night** to **weekend**.

_____

_____

_____

_____

_____

_____

_____

_____

Building Vocabulary and Spelling

Learning Words with the Sound of i in fish *

i = f i s h   This sound is usually spelled with the letter **i** and others.

fish

bridge

Activity 13 **Which Words Do You Know?**

This list has 45 words with the sound of **i** in f**i**sh.

1. Notice the spelling patterns.

2. Check ✓ the words you know.

3. Look up new words in a dictionary. Write the meanings in your Vocabulary Notebook.

Common Words

GROUP 1:
Words spelled with **i**

☐ **1.** b i g

☐ **2.** b r i d g e

☐ **3.** c h i c k e n

☐ **4.** c i t y

☐ **5.** d e l i c i o u s

☐ **6.** d i d

☐ **7.** d i f f e r e n t

☐ **8.** d i f f i c u l t

☐ **9.** d i n n e r

☐ **10.** d r i n k**

☐ **11.** f i s h

☐ **12.** g i v e

☐ **13.** h i m

☐ **14.** h i s

☐ **15.** i f

☐ **16.** i n

☐ **17.** i n t e r e s t i n g

☐ **18.** i s

☐ **19.** i t

☐ **20.** k i t c h e n

*List is from: Spelling Vocabulary List © 2013 Keith Folse
Note: The vowel in the letters –ink** (e.g., in the word **drink**) may sound like the **e** in h**e** or **eat** to some speakers.

☐ **21.** l i s t

☐ **22.** l i t t l e

☐ **23.** l i v e

☐ **24.** m i l k

☐ **25.** m i n u t e

☐ **26.** p i n k*

☐ **27.** r i n g

☐ **28.** s i c k

☐ **29.** s i n g

☐ **30.** s i s t e r

☐ **31.** s i t

☐ **32.** s i x

☐ **33.** s w i m

☐ **34.** t h i n g

☐ **35.** t h i n k*

☐ **36.** t h i s

☐ **37.** w h i c h

☐ **38.** w i l l

☐ **39.** w i n

☐ **40.** w i n t e r

☐ **41.** w i t h

GROUP 2:
Other spellings

☐ **42.** p r e t t y

☐ **43.** b e e n

☐ **44.** w o m e n

☐ **45.** b u s y

*Note: The vowel in the letters –**ink** (e.g., in the words **pink** and **think**) may sound like the **e** in h**e** or **eat** to some speakers.

ACTIVITY 14 **Matching Words and Pictures**

Use the list in Activity 13 to write the common word that matches the picture.

1. _____

3. _____

2. _____

4. _____

5. _____

7. _____

6. _____

8. _____

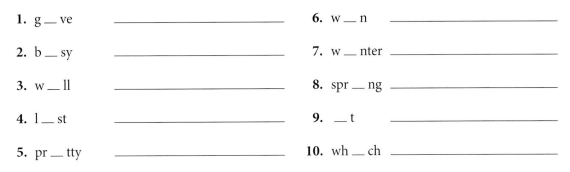

ACTIVITY 15 **Spelling Words with the Sound of i̲ in fi̲sh.**

Fill in the missing letters to spell words with the sound of **i** in fi̲sh. Then copy the correct word.

1. g __ ve _____

2. b __ sy _____

3. w __ ll _____

4. l __ st _____

5. pr __ tty _____

6. w __ n _____

7. w __ nter _____

8. spr __ ng _____

9. __ t _____

10. wh __ ch _____

ACTIVITY 16 **Writing Sentences with Vocabulary in Context**

Complete each sentence with the correct word from Activity 15. Then copy the sentence with correct capital letters and end punctuation.

1. .... car do you like

_____

2. can you .... me a different book

_____

3. i want to .... the football match tomorrow

_____

4. all the plants are green in ....

_____

5. the weather can be very cold in ....

_____

6. here is a .... of things we need for dinner

_____

7. everybody in our office is so .... today

_____

8. we .... take a big exam tomorrow

_____

9. those roses are really ....

_____

10. my english class has eight men and ten .... in it

_____

ACTIVITY 17 **Scrambled Letters**

Change the order of the letters to write a word that has the sound of **i** in f**i**sh.

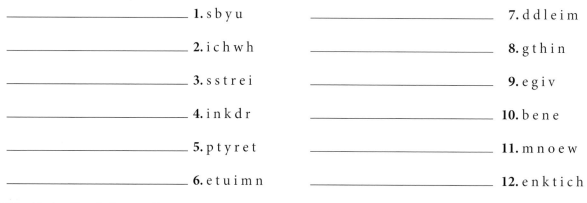

_____ **1.** s b y u   _____ **7.** d d l e i m

_____ **2.** i c h w h   _____ **8.** g t h i n

_____ **3.** s s t r e i   _____ **9.** e g i v

_____ **4.** i n k d r   _____ **10.** b e n e

_____ **5.** p t y r e t   _____ **11.** m n o e w

_____ **6.** e t u i m n   _____ **12.** e n k t i c h

ACTIVITY 18 Spelling Practice

Write the word that you hear. You will hear each word two times.

1. _____   6. _____   11. _____

2. _____   7. _____   12. _____

3. _____   8. _____   13. _____

4. _____   9. _____   14. _____

5. _____   10. _____   15. _____

ACTIVITY 19 Spelling Review: Which Word Is Correct?

This review covers the different ways of spelling the sound of **i** in f**i**sh in this unit. Read each pair of words. Circle the word that is spelled correctly.

	A	B		A	B
1.	chicken	checkin	11.	sing	seng
2.	did	ded	12.	sitt	sit
3.	pritty	pretty	13.	thnk	think
4.	ben	been	14.	hes	his
5.	giv	give	15.	intrsting	interesting
6.	if	ife	16.	little	littl
7.	list	liste	17.	dennir	dinner
8.	city	sity	18.	swime	swim
9.	big	bigg	19.	bisy	busy
10.	liv	live	20.	women	womin

Read the four words in each row. Underline the word that is spelled correctly.

	A	B	C	D
1.	denner	dinnr	denner	dinner
2.	limun	limon	lemon	lemin
3.	esimple	simple	semble	semple
4.	frind	frend	freind	friend
5.	bein	been	bn	ben
6.	everything	evrithing	everythng	evrithng
7.	swem	eswem	eswim	swim
8.	niver	nivr	never	nivr
9.	happan	hapen	happen	happin
10.	bisy	busy	buesy	bissy
11.	neaxt	nixt	nxt	next
12.	minute	menit	minit	menute
13.	pik	pick	bik	bick
14.	egain	agen	again	agin
15.	ridy	redy	rady	ready
16.	letle	littl	little	litl
17.	winter	wnter	wintir	wentir
18.	enstead	instead	ensted	insted
19.	Jenuary	January	Jinuary	Jonuary
20.	laugh	leagh	lagh	laf

Original Student Writing

Writing Your Ideas in Sentences or a Paragraph

Write five to ten sentences on your own paper. Write about things that people usually do. Use simple present tense. For help, you can follow the examples in Activity 12 (page 34) for one person or Activity 11 (page 33) for two or more people.

Peer Editing

Exchange papers from the above activity. Read your partner's sentences. Then use Peer Editing Sheet 1 on ELTNGL.com/sites/els to make comments about the writing.

NOTES

CAREER PATHS 3

Astronaut Samantha
Cristoforetti takes photos
from the International
Space Station.

THINK AND DISCUSS

1 What was your dream job when you were
a child?

2 What is your dream job now? Is it different?

A **Look at the information on these pages and answer the questions.**

1. In which places is engineer the top dream job?
2. What are the top dream jobs for men and women in the United States?
3. What percentage of people say that they have their dream job?

B **Match the correct form of the words in blue to their definitions.**

_____ (n) something you really want to happen

_____ (adj) wanting to know about something

_____ (v) to succeed in doing something

Canada

United States

Brazil

DREAM JOBS

What was your **dream** job when you were a child? The website LinkedIn asked 8,000 working people from around the world this question. The top five dream jobs were: engineer, airplane pilot, doctor / nurse, scientist, and teacher.

It also seems that men and women were **interested in** very different jobs as children. In the United States, for example, the top five dream jobs for men were completely different from the dream jobs for women.

But how many people actually **achieved** their dream job? According to the survey, 30 percent of people have their dream job now, or they have a job that is similar to it.

Top dream jobs in the U.S.

Women	Men
1 Teacher	1 Athlete
2 Veterinarian	2 Pilot
3 Writer	3 Scientist
4 Doctor / Nurse	4 Lawyer
5 Singer	5 Astronaut

Sweden

France

Germany

United Arab Emirates

India

Hong Kong, China

Singapore

Indonesia

South Africa

Australia

New Zealand

Number one dream job (women and men)

Engineer   Pilot   Doctor / Nurse   Scientist   Teacher

Reading 1 QUICK READ SEE PAGE 116

PREPARING TO READ

BUILDING
VOCABULARY

A The words in **blue** below are used in the reading passage on pages 48–49. Match each word with its definition.

A job as an airline pilot is a dream for many people. But if you **plan** to become an airline pilot, here are a few things you should know:

- It helps to be **smart**, and you also need a good college degree.
- Training to be a pilot is **expensive**. Some pilots pay more than $100,000 for their training.
- If you get a job with an airline **company**, you need to **practice** in a simulator for about a month before you can **begin** to fly.
- The money is good, though. Many airline pilots **earn** over $100,000 a year.

1. _____ (v) to start

2. _____ (n) a business that makes money by selling products or services

3. _____ (v) to receive money for working

4. _____ (adj) costing a lot of money

5. _____ (v) to do something so that you get better at it

6. _____ (adj) able to learn things quickly and easily

7. _____ (v) to think about what you will do in the future

USING
VOCABULARY

B List three ideas for each category below. Then share your ideas with a partner.

1. three jobs where people **earn** a lot of money

   _____   _____   _____

2. three big **companies** from your country

   _____   _____   _____

3. three people who you think are really **smart**

   _____   _____   _____

A Korean Air passenger plane lands in the Czech Republic.

DEVELOPING READING SKILLS

READING SKILL Skimming

When you skim a reading passage, you look at it quickly before you start to read it. Skimming helps you to predict—or guess—what the reading is about. It helps you to understand ideas better when you read the passage more carefully later.

Parts of a passage you can skim are the following:

- **Pictures and captions** (Captions are the words that explain the pictures. They are usually below or next to the pictures.)
- **The title** (It can tell you a lot about a passage.)
- **Subheadings** (These are the titles of different sections of a reading.)
- **The first and last sentences of paragraphs** (You often find the main ideas in these sentences.)

A Look at the picture and read the caption on pages 48–49. Answer these questions: SKIMMING

1. Who is the passage about? _____

2. What job do you think the person has? _____

B Now read the title of the passage on page 48 and answer this question: SKIMMING

Reaching for the sky is an expression that usually means "trying to achieve a goal." What goals do you think Barrington Irving had?

_____

_____

C Next, read the subheads in the passage and answer these questions: SKIMMING

1. How does Barrington Irving feel about flying?

_____

2. Where do you think he wanted to fly?

_____

D Now read the first paragraph. What challenges do you think Irving faced? Note your ideas below.   PREDICTING

_____

_____

_____

E Now read the whole passage and check your ideas in **D**.

REACHING FOR THE SKY

A   In 2007, Barrington Irving became the youngest person to fly solo[1] around the world. He was just 23 years old—and he built the plane himself. How did he achieve this?

A PASSION FOR FLYING

B   Irving's interest in flying started when he was 15. He was working in his parents' bookstore in Miami, Florida. One of the customers[2] was a pilot, Gary Robinson. One day, Robinson asked Irving if he was interested in flying. Irving didn't think he was smart enough. But the next day, Robinson took Irving to an airport. He showed Irving inside the cockpit[3] of a Boeing 777. That experience changed Irving's life.

Irving really wanted to fly, but flight school was **expensive**. To achieve his dream, he worked different jobs. He washed airplanes and cleaned swimming pools. At home, he **practiced** flying on a video game. In the end, he **earned** enough money for flight school.

CIRCLING THE WORLD

At flight school, Irving achieved his **dream** of learning how to fly. But he wasn't finished. Next, he **planned** to build his own plane and fly solo around the world.

Barrington Irving and his plane, *Inspiration*

Building the plane was difficult. Irving asked more than 50 **companies** for airplane parts. Most said no, but he kept asking. Three years later, he had parts worth $300,000. Columbia, an airplane company, agreed to build a plane using the parts. Soon, his airplane was ready to fly.

On March 23, 2007, Irving **began** his round-the-world trip. After 97 days—with 145 hours in the air—he landed back in Miami. A cheering crowd of people was there to welcome him.

SHARING THE DREAM

Irving saw many young people in the crowd, and this had a powerful effect on him. He wanted to use his experience to help other young people achieve their own dreams.

"Everyone told me what I couldn't do," says Irving. "They said I was too young, that I didn't have enough money. [But] even if no one believes in your dream," he says, "you have to pursue it."

[1]If you do something **solo**, you do it alone.
[2]**Customers** are people who buy things.
[3]The **cockpit** of a plane is the place where the pilot sits.

EXPERIENCE AVIATION

In 2005, Barrington Irving founded Experience Aviation. The organization uses aviation—the designing, building, and flying of aircraft—to build students' skills in science, technology, engineering, and math. In this way, it hopes to inspire young people to achieve dream jobs in aviation or similar industries.

UNDERSTANDING THE READING

UNDERSTANDING THE GIST

A Which of the following would be the best alternative title for the passage?

a. How to Build Your Own Plane   b. Achieving a Dream   c. Life in Flight School

UNDERSTANDING A SEQUENCE

B Put the events (a–f) in the correct order. Write the correct number (1–6) next to each event.

___3___ a. Irving learned to fly.

_____ b. Irving met Gary Robinson.

_____ c. Irving flew around the world.

_____ d. Irving got the parts for his plane.

_____ e Irving decided to build a plane and fly around the world.

_____ f. Irving went to the airport and saw the inside of an airplane.

UNDERSTANDING DETAILS

C Circle the correct options to answer the questions.

1. Why was Gary Robinson important in Irving's life?
   a. He taught Irving how to fly.   b. He got Irving interested in flying.

2. How did Irving get enough money for flight school?
   a. He worked different jobs.   b. He asked a company for money.

3. How did Irving get the parts for his airplane?
   a. He asked many different companies.   b. He built them himself.

4. What is the main aim of Experience Aviation?
   a. to teach people how airplanes work   b. to help young people get a dream job

CRITICAL THINKING: GUESSING MEANING FROM CONTEXT

D Find and underline the following words in the reading on pages 48–49. Use the context to help you understand the meaning.

parts (paragraph E)   **cheering** (paragraph F)   **pursue** (paragraph H)

Write the correct form of each word next to its definition. Check your answers in a dictionary.

1. _____ to try to reach or achieve something

2. _____ to shout happily

3. _____ a piece of a machine

> **CRITICAL THINKING**   **Inferring** means understanding something that the writer does not say directly. When you make inferences about a person, for example, you guess information about that person by the things they do.

CRITICAL THINKING: INFERRING

E From the reading passage, what can we infer about Barrington Irving's character? Find and underline at least three sentences in the passage that support your opinion.

Video

CAVE SCIENTIST

Geologist Gina Moseley inside a cave in Greenland

BEFORE VIEWING

A Look at the photo and the title of the video. What do you think Gina Moseley's job is like? Discuss your ideas with a partner.

PREDICTING

B Read the paragraph. The words in **bold** are used in the video. Match each word with the correct definition.

VOCABULARY IN CONTEXT

A geologist is someone who studies rocks. It's a **challenging** job, as geologists often travel to **remote** places. By studying rocks, geologists can learn a lot about the past. For example, rocks can tell us about past **climate change**. This information is **valuable** because it helps us understand what might happen in the future.

1. _____ (adj) far away from cities and towns

2. _____ (adj) very useful or important

3. _____ (n) changes in the Earth's weather over time

4. _____ (adj) difficult but interesting

C Read the information about Greenland. Then answer the questions.

Five facts about Greenland
- Greenland is the largest island in the world, but only around 57,000 people live there.
- 15,000 people live in the capital city, Nuuk.
- Greenland is not very green. Around 80 percent of the island is covered in ice and snow.
- From May 25th to July 25th, the sun does not go down in some parts of Greenland.
- It's a difficult place to get around. There are only about 63 kilometers of road in the whole country.

1. Would you like to visit Greenland? Why or why not?

   _____

2. Do you think Greenland is a good place for geologists to work? Why or why not?

   _____

WHILE VIEWING

A ▶ What does Moseley say about her job? Watch the video once and check (✓) the correct answers.

☐ 1. She goes to places that very few people have visited.

☐ 2. She enjoys the long journey to the caves.

☐ 3. She enjoys working as part of a team.

☐ 4. She's happy that the work she does is important.

B ▶ Watch the video a second time and answer the questions.

1. When did Moseley first become interested in caves?

   _____

2. How long does it take to get to the caves?

   _____

3. What can the cave rocks tell us about past climate change?

   _____

AFTER VIEWING

A Complete the chart with information about Gina Moseley's job.

Good Things	Challenges

B Would you like Moseley's job? Why or why not? Discuss with a partner.

Reading 2 QUICK READ SEE PAGE 119

PREPARING TO READ

A The words in **blue** below are used in the reading passage on pages 54–56. Match the correct form of each word to its definition.

BUILDING VOCABULARY

One day, Canadian street entertainer Guy Laliberté had an **idea**. Would it be **possible**, he wondered, to get all the street entertainers he knew to perform **together** in one big **show**? Laliberté started a company that later became known as Cirque du Soleil, or "Circus of the Sun." The show **soon** became very popular. Now it **travels** to different countries, and is **perhaps** the most famous circus in the world. Millions of people have seen a Cirque du Soleil show, and people often **return** to see the shows many times.

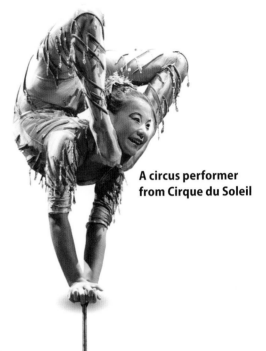

A circus performer from Cirque du Soleil

1. _____ (n) a thought about something

2. _____ (adv) with other people

3. _____ (v) to go back to a place again

4. _____ (adv) in a short time

5. _____ (adv) maybe

6. _____ (v) to move from one place to another

7. _____ (adj) able to be done

8. _____ (n) a performance (e.g., of dance or music)

B Answer the questions. Then share your ideas with a partner.

USING VOCABULARY

1. When was the last time you saw a **show**? What was it?

   _____

2. Would you **return** to see the show again? Why or why not?

   _____

C Skim the reading passage on pages 54–56. Which of the following best describes Emily Ainsworth? Check your ideas as you read the passage.

PREDICTING

   a. a street entertainer who joined Mexico's most famous circus
   b. a dancer who started a successful traveling circus in Mexico
   c. a photographer who was able to spend time in a Mexican circus

LIFE IN THE RING

A   As a child, Emily Ainsworth loved the colorful world of traveling circuses. As she grew older, she also became interested in other cultures. "England is a small country," she says. "I saved up for years . . . so that I could afford to travel abroad."

B   Ainsworth had many different jobs to pay for her travels. When she was 16, she had earned enough money to travel to Mexico. The experience changed her life. She fell in love with the country and dreamed that perhaps she could return one day.

C   As a 22-year-old, Ainsworth got her chance. She entered a radio competition to think of an interesting travel idea. The winner would go on the journey and make a documentary.[1] Ainsworth's idea was to go to Mexico to learn about the lives of circus workers. To her surprise, she won the competition.

D   Mexico has many circuses. One of the smaller ones is Circo Padilla. Soon after arriving in Mexico, Ainsworth met Padilla's ringmaster,[2] Don Humberto. He invited her to visit his circus.

E   On her first day in Circo Padilla, one of the dancers could not take part in the show.

Humberto asked Ainsworth if she wanted to be a dancer. Five minutes later, Ainsworth says, she was wearing dancer's clothes. It was, she says, "like a childhood dream come true."

F   As a circus dancer, Ainsworth and the other circus workers performed and lived together. She also studied and took pictures of circus life. The days were quiet, but at night, the circus world came alive.

G   Ainsworth now has a career as a journalist[3] and photographer. She still has a love for Mexico and returns there when she can. "I still feel like a part of that world," she says.

H   Her advice to young people is to follow their childhood dreams. "When you're eight years old," she says, "you know that anything is possible."

[1] A **documentary** is a film or TV show about real people or real situations.
[2] A **ringmaster** is the leader of a circus.
[3] A **journalist** writes for a newspaper or magazine.

Emily Ainsworth (right) with a circus performer in Mexico

A pair of Chilean trapeze artists performs in Circo Atayde, a traveling Mexican circus.

UNDERSTANDING THE READING

UNDERSTANDING MAIN IDEAS

A Write the correct paragraph letter (A, B, C, E, F) from the reading next to its main idea.

_____ 1. Ainsworth got the chance to return to Mexico.

_____ 2. Ainsworth performed in the circus and studied circus life.

_____ 3. Ainsworth was interested in learning about other cultures from an early age.

_____ 4. Ainsworth's first trip to Mexico changed her life.

_____ 5. Ainsworth got the chance to be a circus dancer.

UNDERSTANDING DETAILS

B Complete the sentences with details from the reading. Write the correct paragraph letter from exercise **A** next to each detail.

Supporting Idea   **Paragraph**

1. To save money to go to Mexico the first time, Ainsworth _____

   _____   _____

2. Ainsworth got the chance to go to Mexico again because she

   _____   _____

3. When she was not performing, Ainsworth _____

   _____   _____

CRITICAL THINKING: GUESSING MEANING FROM CONTEXT

C Find and underline the following words in the reading. Use the context to help you understand the meaning. Then write the correct form of each word or phrase next to its definition.

   abroad (paragraph A)   **performed** (paragraph F)   **came alive** (paragraph F)

   1. _____ (v) to dance or sing for other people

   2. _____ (v) to become exciting

   3. _____ (adv) in or to a different country

CRITICAL THINKING: SYNTHESIZING

D Note answers to the questions below. Then discuss with a partner.

1. In what ways are Barrington Irving and Emily Ainsworth similar?

   _____

2. Whose dream would you like to follow more—Irving's or Ainsworth's? Why?

   _____

Writing

EXPLORING WRITTEN ENGLISH

A Read the information below.

> ### LANGUAGE FOR WRITING Verbs + Infinitives
>
> When certain verbs are followed by other verbs, the infinitive form (*to* + verb) is used.
>
> > Emily Ainsworth **plans to return** to Mexico someday.
> >
> > He **hopes to save** enough money for college.
> >
> > We **want to visit** China next year.
> >
> > I **need to get** a different job.
>
> Verbs that follow *plan, hope, want*, and *need* are usually in the infinitive form. There are many other verbs that follow the same pattern.
>
> Note:
>
> - Infinitive forms do not change—they stay the same for every subject. You never need to add -*s* or -*ing* to an infinitive.
>
> - Always include *to* with the verb.

Now complete the sentences (1–8) with the correct form of the verbs in the box. Use each set of verbs only once.

hope / get	plan / go	plan / graduate	need / take
want / help	need / learn	hope / visit	want / be

1. Many college students _____ a good job after they graduate.

2. We _____ some Spanish before we move to Spain.

3. My sister _____ to flight school because she wants to be a pilot.

4. You and Lisa _____ three more classes.

5. Barrington Irving _____ young people achieve their dreams.

6. My brother _____ from college in three years.

7. I really _____ Mexico someday.

8. He's studying at flight school because he _____ a pilot in the future.

B Talk to your classmates and find someone who *wants*, *hopes*, *plans*, or *needs* to do each of the activities in the chart. Ask for extra information.

Find someone who ...	Name	Extra information
1. wants to learn a new language.		Which language?
2. hopes to become famous one day.		Famous for what?
3. plans to move to another country.		Which country?
4. needs to save money for something.		What for?

Example: A: *Do you want to learn a new language?*

B: *Yes, I do.*

A: *Which language?*

B: *French.*

C Use the information in the chart to write four sentences.

Example: Paul wants to learn French.

_____

_____

_____

_____

EDITING PRACTICE

Read the information below.

In sentences with infinitives, remember:

• Infinitive forms do not change—they stay the same for every subject. You never need to add *-s* or *-ing* to an infinitive.

• Always include *to*.

Find and correct one mistake in each of the sentences (1–5).

1. I want get a job in France this summer.

2. Irving plans to helps young people who want to become pilots.

3. Some chefs need studying another language to work in restaurants overseas.

4. Lara hopes become famous one day.

5. My friend wants to having a party.

Collocations are words that go together in phrases. It's a good idea to learn collocations as set phrases.

Here are some collocations for talking about hopes, plans, and dreams:

verbs	nouns
go	*to college / to university*
take	*a class / a vacation*
finish	*school / college*
start	*a new job / a family*
learn	*a language / the piano*
study	*math / French*

D Circle the noun or noun phrase that does NOT collocate with the verb.

1. **go**   a. to flight school   b. to Europe   c. a new job
2. **take**   a. a trip   b. school   c. an exam
3. **finish**   a. a language   b. university   c. a project
4. **start**   a. university   b. a business   c. history
5. **learn**   a. a class   b. the guitar   c. how to fly
6. **study**   a. science   b. a class   c. English

E Complete each sentence with a suitable verb. Sometimes more than one verb is possible.

1. To be a doctor, he needs to _____ a medical exam.

2. My sister hopes to _____ a language so she can work overseas.

3. Before I buy a car, I need to _____ how to drive.

4. I hope to be a circus performer in Mexico, so I plan to _____ a class in Spanish.

5. My friend wants to be a pilot, so she plans to _____ to college and study aviation.

6. After he _____ college, my brother wants to _____ a business.

F Correct each sentence below by replacing one word.

1. I hope to take to university after I finish high school.

2. I want to start French when I go to college.

3. My friend plans to go to Asia after he passes university.

4. If I want to pass my math exam, I think I need to study an extra class.

WRITING TASK

GOAL You are going to write sentences on the following topic:
Describe your plans and dreams for the future.

PLANNING **A** Follow the steps to plan your writing. Make notes in the chart.

Step 1 Write down three dreams or plans that you have for the future.

Step 2 List the things that you need to do to achieve each dream or plan.

My Plan/Dream:	To achieve this, I need to:
1.	
2.	
3.	

FIRST DRAFT **B** Use your ideas above to write three pairs of sentences. In each pair, describe your plan or dream, and explain what you need to do to achieve it. Use *plan*, *want*, *hope*, and *need* and the collocations for achieving dreams.

Example:

I hope to travel around the world after I finish college.

I plan to get a part-time job because I need to save a lot of money.

EDITING **C** Now edit your draft. Correct mistakes with *plan*, *want*, *hope*, and *need* and the collocations for achieving dreams. Use the checklist on page 124.

UNIT REVIEW

Answer the following questions.

1. What was the most interesting job in this unit? Why?

_____

_____

2. What are two collocations with the verb *take*?

_____

3. What are two collocations with the verb *finish*?

_____

4. Do you remember the meanings of these words? Check (✔) the ones you know. Look back at the unit and review the ones you don't know.

Reading 1:

☐ achieve AWL   ☐ begin   ☐ company
☐ dream   ☐ earn   ☐ expensive
☐ interested in   ☐ plan   ☐ practice
☐ smart

Reading 2:

☐ idea   ☐ perhaps   ☐ possible
☐ return   ☐ show   ☐ soon
☐ together   ☐ travel

NOTES

Writing about the Present

Young Rajasthani girls carry water across
the desert near Jaisalmer, India.

OBJECTIVES To learn the simple present tense
To study simple and compound sentences
To practice the articles *a* and *an*

Can you write about things you do every day?

The Simple Present Tense: Statements

Use the **simple present tense** to write about:

- daily habits or routines

  Max checks his e-mail each morning.

- general truths

  Children go to school.

  Fish live in water.

Be	
I **am**	we **are**
you **are**	you (plural) **are**
he / she / it **is**	they **are**

Visit / Leave / Carry	
I **visit** **leave** **carry**	we **visit** **leave** **carry**
you **visit** **leave** **carry**	you (plural) **visit** **leave** **carry**
he / she / it **visits** **leaves** **carries**	they **visit** **leave** **carry**

Have	
I **have**	we **have**
you **have**	you (plural) **have**
he / she / it **has**	they **have**

IMPORTANT: Verbs for third person singular subjects (*he, she, it, Nick, Sylvia*) end in **–s** or **–es**.

✗ He call his parents every day.

✓ He calls his parents every day.

✗ I be a student.

✗ I is a student.

✓ I am a student.

✗ He have homework every day.

✓ He has homework every day.

✓ We have homework every day.

ACTIVITY 1 **Practicing the Simple Present Tense**

Fill in the blanks with the correct simple present tense form of the verb in parentheses.

Uncle Charlie and Aunt Valerie

My Uncle Charlie and Aunt Valerie (**1.** be) _____

successful entrepreneurs. Their restaurant (**2.** be) _____

ten years old now, and they (**3.** enjoy) _____ great success.

The restaurant (**4.** have) _____ 15 servers, two managers,

and three chefs. Uncle Charlie (**5.** work) _____ very

hard in his restaurant. Sometimes he (**6.** be) _____ there

seven days a week. Aunt Valerie always (**7.** go) _____

to the restaurant at night to make sure that the customers (**8.** be)

_____ happy. I (**9.** love) _____ my Uncle

Charlie and Aunt Valerie, and I really appreciate all their hard work.

There (**10.** be) _____ no one better than them!

ACTIVITY 2 **Practicing the Simple Present Tense**

Fill in the blanks with the correct simple present form of the verbs in the word bank. Some verbs may be used more than once.

love	play	be	speak	come	practice	have

My Classmates

My classmates come from all over the world. José

1 _____ from Spain, so he **2** _____

Spanish perfectly. Wonbin and Hyun-Ju **3** _____

Korean, but they **4** _____ from different cities. Yuri

5 _____ from Ukraine. He **6** _____

English all the time and **7** _____ a great accent. The

Al-Ahmad brothers **8** _____ from Dubai, and they

9 _____ soccer very well. What about me? I

10 _____ from Italy, and I **11** _____ to

sing in class. We **12** _____ all very good friends, and I

hope we can be friends forever.

ACTIVITY 3 Ordering Sentences in a Paragraph

Number the sentences in the correct paragraph order.

Jim's Daily Routine

_____ a. After this part-time job, he goes home, eats a quick dinner, studies, and does his homework.

___2___ b. He studies engineering at City College.

_____ c. He goes to school for six hours.

_____ d. Jim knows that this lifestyle is stressful.

___1___ e. Jim is a very busy student.

_____ f. Every morning, he wakes up at 7:00, takes a shower, and then rushes off to school.

_____ g. He also knows that the stress will end soon, and he will get a professional job.

_____ h. After school, he goes to the local mall where he works in a sporting goods store.

ACTIVITY 4 Changing Singular Verbs to Plural Verbs

Make the following changes to the sentences in Activity 3, and rewrite the paragraph in the correct order.

1. Change the subject of the story from *Jim* to *Jim and Matt*.

2. Make any necessary changes to verb forms, nouns, and pronouns.

Example Paragraph 3

Jim and Matt's Daily Routine

Jim and Matt are very busy students.

_____

_____

_____

_____

_____

_____

_____

_____

_____

_____

Writer's Note

Using Contractions

A contraction is a shortened form of two words combined with an apostrophe (').
The apostrophe takes the place of the missing letter.

I am = I'm   we are = we're

you are = you're   you (plural) are = you're

he is = he's / she is = she's / it is = it's   they are = they're

Contractions are often used in informal writing. Ask your instructor if using contractions in your academic writing is acceptable in your class.

ACTIVITY 5   Editing: Subjects and Verbs

Correct the paragraph. There are 7 mistakes. The first mistake has been corrected for you.

2 missing subjects   5 missing verbs

Example Paragraph 4

The City of Budapest

Budapest ^is^ one of the most interesting capitals of Europe. Is a romantic city, and it has many interesting tourist places to visit. One example the Danube River. It separates Budapest into Buda and Pest. In addition, visitors traditional Hungarian food. The most popular food goulash soup. The people of Budapest friendly and helpful to tourists. When travel to Europe, you can visit Budapest and have a very good time.

Study the pictures on page 68. They tell a story. Then read the incomplete paragraph. Fill in the blanks based on the pictures. You may need to add two or more words in each blank. Write the full sentence for the last two sentences. NOTE: The numbers in the paragraph correspond to the pictures.

Example Paragraph 5

One Family's Morning Routine

The Lee family is very busy on weekday mornings. **1** Every morning Susan Lee, the oldest daughter, wakes up and _____ for her parents and siblings. She loves to cook in the mornings! **2** When the food is ready, the rest of the family _____ . The kids eat their breakfast quickly. **3** After they eat, Susan's father and mother _____ . **4** At 8:30 A.M., Mr. Lee _____ and sees that it is time to leave. **5** Then he and the kids _____ to Mrs. Lee. **6** Mr. Lee and the kids _____ the minivan so that he can take them to school.

7 _____

8 A few minutes later, _____ .

The Lees certainly do a lot before their work and school day begins!

Grammar for Writing

There Is / There Are

Use **There is** and **There are** to show that something exists in a certain place. Use *is* with singular subjects. Use *are* with plural subjects.

There	Is / Are	Subject	(Place Phrase)
There	**is**	a magazine	on the table.
There	**is**	milk	in the refrigerator.
There	**are**	magazines	at the library.
There	**are**	yellow birds.	

✗ There is ten people in my office.
✓ There are ten people in my office.

✗ Is a desk in the room.
✓ There is a desk in the room.

✗ Apples on the table.
✓ There are apples on the table.

✗ A concert at the university tomorrow.
✓ There is a concert at the university tomorrow.

Study the four examples of *there is* and *there are* in the paragraph below. Then answer the questions.

Example Paragraph 6

My Colorful Classroom

My classroom is a very colorful room. **1** *There are* twenty desks in the room. Each desk has a dark brown seat and a shiny white top. On the left side of the room, **2** *there is* a world map. This map shows all the different countries in the world, and each country is a different color. On the right side of the room, **3** *there are* two posters. The first poster is green. It has a list of fifty common verbs. The second poster has the names and pictures of fruits and vegetables. It is white, but the writing is black. Finally, **4** *there are* some pictures of famous leaders above the whiteboard. These objects make my classroom colorful.

Post-Reading

1. Is example 1 singular or plural? _____ Why? _____

2. Is example 2 singular or plural? _____ Why? _____

3. Is example 3 singular or plural? _____ Why? _____

4. Is example 4 singular or plural? _____ Why? _____

5. Is there a map in the room? _____ Where? _____

6. Is there a calendar in the room? _____ Where? _____

7. Is there a cat in the room? _____ Where? _____

8. Are there pictures of people in the room? _____ Where? _____

ACTIVITY 8 Using *There Is / There Are*

Write ten sentences about the objects in the picture of the living room. Use *there is* and *there are*. You may use the words in the box to help you.

bookshelf	picture	television	TV console	couch
pillows	coffee table	chair	rug	vase
bowl	watch	magazines	remote control	books

1. _____

2. _____

3. _____

4. _____

5. _____

6. _____

7. _____

8. _____

9. _____

10. _____

ACTIVITY 9 Editing Practice

The paragraph below has four mistakes with verbs and *There is / There are*. Circle and correct the mistakes. Then explain your corrections.

Example Paragraph 7

The English Alphabet

There have 26 letters in the English alphabet. There is five vowel letters and 21 consonant letters. The five vowels are *a, e, i, o,* and *u.* The letters *w* and *y* can be vowels when they come after other vowels. There three letters with the *a* sound in their names. These letters are *a, j,* and *k.* Are nine letters with the *e* sound in their names. These are *b, c, d, e, g, p, t, v,* and *z.* If you want to speak English well, you have to learn the 26 letters of the English alphabet.

1. _____

2. _____

3. _____

4. _____

Writer's Note

There are vs. They are

Be careful not to confuse *There are* and *They are.*

- **There are** shows that something exists in a particular location. The subject of the sentence comes after *are* (*There are* + subject).

- **They are** is the beginning of a sentence about a group of people or things. The subject of the sentence is *They.*

    ✗ <u>They</u> are five people in my family.

    ✓ There are five people in my family.

    ✗ Piano keys have two colors. <u>There</u> are black and white.

    ✓ Piano keys have two colors. They are black and white.

ACTIVITY 10 Practicing *They Are* vs. *There Are*

Fill in the blanks with *There are* or *They are.*

1. _____ too many questions on this test!

2. _____ happy to see us today.

3. _____ at the doctor.

4. _____ many different ways to study English.

5. _____ some apples in the kitchen.

6. _____ at the store right now.

7. _____ my best friends in the whole world.

8. _____ two servers in the restaurant.

9. _____ great teachers at our school.

10. _____ excited about Mark's party.

ACTIVITY 11 Editing: Capitalization Review

Correct the paragraph. There are 11 capitalization mistakes. The first mistake has been corrected for you.

Example Paragraph 8

Amazing Tourist Towers

Did you know that many popular travel spots are former
                                                  T
World's **Fair** towers? The most famous is the Eiffel ~~t~~ower from the
1889 fair in paris. This tall **graceful** tower is a well-known symbol of
france. Tourists often ride boats on the Seine river at night and look
at the tower's beautiful lights. Another famous fair tower is in seattle,

a fair: an outdoor entertainment event with rides, games, and displays

graceful: moving in a smooth and beautiful way

73

Washington, in the united States. The space Needle comes from the 1962 World's Fair, and it looks like a giant tower with a **UFO** on top of it. people love to eat in the **revolving** restaurant at the top. In Daejeon, South korea, travelers love to visit the Tower of grand Light from the 1993 World's Fair. This silver and red tower is now part of a giant amusement park where people can swim, watch movies, and enjoy exciting rides. These are only a few of the amazing tourist **destinations** that have their beginnings in the world's Fair!

a UFO: an alien space ship or "unidentified flying object"

revolving: moving in a circle

a destination: a place you travel to

Grammar for Writing

The Simple Present Tense: Negative Statements

To make negative statements with *be,* add *not* after *am/is/are.*

Be (Negative)	
I **am** <u>**not**</u>	we **are** <u>**not**</u>
you **are** <u>**not**</u>	you (plural) **are** <u>**not**</u>
he / she / it **is** <u>**not**</u>	they **are** <u>**not**</u>
✗ You <u>not</u> at school today.	
✓ You are not at school today.	

NOTE: You can form contractions with *is/are* and *not.*

is not = isn't   are not = aren't

there is not = there isn't   there are not = there aren't

To make negative statements with other verbs, use *do not* and *does not.*

I	**do not**	have live go	we	**do not**	have live go
you	**do not**	have live go	you (plural)	**do not**	have live go
he she it	**does not**	have live go	they	**do not**	have live go
✗ Vegetarians <u>not</u> eat meat.					
✓ Vegetarians do not eat meat.					
✗ He <u>do</u> not <u>goes</u> to my school.					
✓ He does not go to my school.					

NOTE: You can form contractions with *do / does* and *not.*

do not = don't   does not = doesn't

ACTIVITY 12   Changing Verbs from Affirmative to Negative

Change the verb in each sentence from the affirmative to the negative. Also write the contraction form.

1. I have a car.

   I do not (don't) have a car.

2. The capital of Japan is Osaka.

   _____

3. Jeremy goes to the library every day.

   _____

4. There is a Thai restaurant on Green Street.

   _____

5. Angel Falls is in Brazil.

   _____

6. Kate and Julia are roommates.

_____

7. Jeff and Michael work at the gas station.

_____

8. There are answers in the back of the book.

_____

9. The teacher wants a new computer.

_____

10. Olivia bakes cookies every Saturday.

_____

ACTIVITY 13 **Practicing Possessive Adjectives**

Think about the answers to these questions. Then write the answers using complete sentences.
Use a possessive adjective three times.

1. What is your best friend's first name?

    My best friend's first name _____

2. What is your best friend's last name?

_____

3. Where is your best friend from?

_____

4. How big is your best friend's family?

_____

5. Why is this person your best friend?

_____

6. What job does your best friend want to do in the future?

_____

ACTIVITY 14 **Writing Information in Paragraph Form**

Write your sentences from Activity 13 in paragraph form. Give your paragraph a title, and remember to indent the first line.

_____

       _____

_____

_____

_____

_____

_____

_____

_____

_____

Grammar for Writing

Simple Sentences

A **simple sentence** is a sentence that has only one subject-verb combination. Most simple sentences have one subject and one verb.

> **Japan** imports oil from Saudi Arabia.

However, simple sentences can have a subject-verb combination that has more than one subject and/or more than one verb.

Subject(s)	Verb(s) + Other information
Japan	imports oil from Saudi Arabia.
Japan and **Germany**	import oil from Saudi Arabia.
Japan	imports oil and exports cars.
Japan and **Germany**	import oil and export cars.
Japan	exports cars and technology.
Japan and **Germany**	export cars and technology.

NOTE: All of these sentences are simple sentences because they have only one subject-verb combination.

Compound Sentences

A **compound sentence** is a sentence that has two simple sentences that are joined by a **connecting word** (such as *and*). A compound sentence has two separate subject-verb combinations.

Subject 1 + Verb 1	Comma	Connecting Word	Subject 2 + Verb 2
Japan imports oil	,	and	**Saudi Arabia** imports vegetables.
Jack likes Italian food	,	but	**he** prefers Thai food.
Abbie watched TV last night	,	so	**she** did not finish her homework.
We can travel to the mountains	,	or	**we** can go to the beach.

IMPORTANT: Compound sentences *always* use a comma (**,**) and a connecting word to connect two sentences.

ACTIVITY 15 Identifying Sentence Types

For each sentence, circle the subject(s) and underline the verb(s). Then write *S* (simple sentence) or *C* (compound sentence).

1. _____C_____ Japan's (flag) is red and white, and Canada's (flag) is also red and white.

2. _____S_____ (Japan and Canada) have the same two colors in their flags.

3. _____ The weather is bad, but the airplane will leave on time.

4. _____ It is extremely hot in Abu Dhabi during the summer.

5. _____ This map of Europe, Africa, and Asia is very old.

6. _____ You can have cake or ice cream for dessert.

7. _____ The students take a test every Friday, but they do not like it!

8. _____ January, March, May, July, August, October, and December have 31 days.

9. _____ This recipe requires two cups of flour, two cups of sugar, and one cup of milk.

10. _____ Ian and Carlos like surfing and skiing.

11. _____ Some people prefer gold rings, but I prefer silver rings.

12. _____ These silver and gold rings are different in weight, so they are different in price.

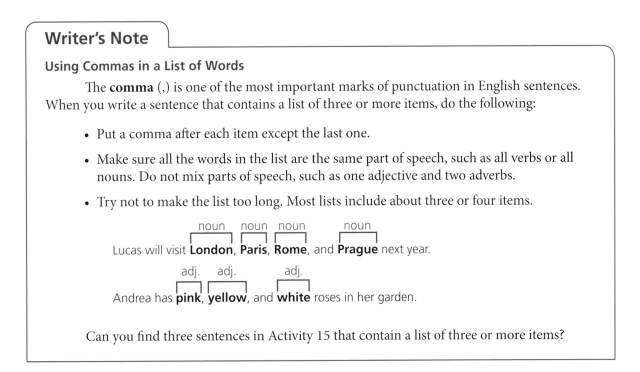
Grammar for Writing

Connecting Words in Compound Sentences

Connecting Word	Meaning	
	1st sentence	**2nd sentence**
and	Gives information.	Adds (similar) information.
but	Gives information.	Adds contrasting (different) information.
so	Tells about something.	Tells about the result of (what happened because of) the event or information in the 1st sentence.
or	Describes a choice (option 1).	Describes another choice (option 2).

Combine each pair of simple sentences into one compound sentence. Use a comma and a connecting word: *and, but, or,* or *so*. Some sentences can be connected with more than one connecting word. Be prepared to explain your choice.

1. Seher lives in Turkey. Seher's sister lives in Canada.

   _____

2. Carlos works on Saturday. He cannot come to the movies with us.

   _____

3. We go to school every day. We play tennis on weekends.

   _____

4. Luis and Kathy are related. They are not brother and sister.

   _____

5. Hurricanes begin in the Atlantic Ocean. Typhoons begin in the Pacific.

   _____

6. I like to go to the beach in the summer. My brother prefers to hike in the mountains.

_____

7. I do not feel well. I will call the doctor.

_____

8. You can watch television. You can watch a movie.

_____

Grammar for Writing

Using *A* and *An* with Count Nouns

A **count noun** is a noun that you can count. A count noun has a singular form (such as *phone*) and a plural form (such as *phones*). A **non-count noun** has only one form (such as *rice*).

Follow these rules for using *a/an* with singular count nouns:

- Use *a* or *an* in front of a singular count noun when the noun is general (not specific).
- Use *a* in front of a singular count noun that begins with a <u>consonant</u> sound.
- Use *an* in front of a singular count noun that begins with a <u>vowel</u> sound.

Non-count Nouns	Count Nouns	
	Singular	**Plural**
money	**a** dollar	twenty dollars
ice	**an** ice cube	ice cubes
information	**a** number	numbers
clothing	**a** blue shirt	blue shirts
vocabulary	**a** word	fifteen words
bread	**a** slice of bread	slices of bread
honesty	**an** honest person	honest people
homework	**an** assignment	three assignments

IMPORTANT: Forgetting to put *a* or *an* in front of a singular count noun is a grammatical mistake.

✗ Will made <u>sandwich</u>.

✓ Will made a sandwich.

✗ There is a bank<u>s</u>.

✓ There is a bank. / There are banks.

✗ Sara has <u>informations</u>.

✗ Sara has <u>an</u> information.

✓ Sara has information.

When there is an adjective before a singular count noun, *a / an* agrees with the first letter of the adjective, not the noun.

   ✗ Our friends attend a̲ excellent school.

   ✓ Our friends attend an excellent school.

   ✗ Erica eats a̲n red apple every day.

   ✓ Erica eats a red apple every day.

ACTIVITY 17   **Using Count and Non-count Nouns**

For each item, decide if the noun is a count noun or a non-count noun. Write *C* (count noun) or *NC* (non-count noun). Then circle all the noun forms that can be used in the sentence below.

This is _____.

1. __C__ (a cat)   cats   a cats   cat

2. __NC__ a ice   an ice   (ice)   ices

3. _____ moneys   a money   money   a moneys

4. _____ breads   bread   a breads   a bread

5. _____ an eraser   a eraser   erasers   an erasers

6. _____ homeworks   a homework   a homeworks   homework

7. _____ an unit   units   a unit   an units

8. _____ country   a country   an country   a countries

9. _____ information   informations   an information   a information

10. _____ a happiness   happiness   happinesses   an happiness

11. _____ word   a word   words   a words

12. _____ an present   a presents   presents   a present

13. _____ a answer   answers   an answers   an answer

14. _____ politician   politicians   a politician   a politicians

ACTIVITY 18   **Using *A* and *An* in Sentences**

Rewrite each sentence. Add *a* or *an* if necessary.

1. My father has stressful job.

   _____

2. You have visitor today.

   _____

3. The teacher gives us homework every day.

   _____

4. There is large cake in the kitchen.

   _____

5. His mother is elegant woman.

   _____

6. I am sorry. I do not have time to talk to you right now.

   _____

7. We take tests in this class every week.

   _____

8. Their sister is great cook!

   _____

9. You can buy good furniture in that store.

   _____

10. This soup needs salt.

   _____

ACTIVITY 19 Editing: Grammar and Sentence Review

Correct the paragraph. There are 13 mistakes. The first mistake has been corrected for you.

2 adjective mistakes	2 verb mistakes	3 capitalization mistakes
2 punctuation mistakes	1 article mistake	2 possessive adjective mistakes
1 subject pronoun mistake		

Example Paragraph 10

Not an Average Teenager

Steven Mills is not your **typical** athletic teenager. Steven is an gymnast, and he want to compete in the olympics. He wakes up at five o'clock in the morning every day because he has to practice before school. First, he has a breakfast healthy. Then she jogs to the National Gymnasium on Cypress street. He practices gymnastics for two hours. Then he gets ready for school. Steven goes to school from eight-thirty in the morning until three o'clock in the afternoon. After school, he returns to the Gymnasium for classes special with him coach. When practice finish at six o'clock, Steven returns home. He eats dinner, does his homework and talks with their family. Steven is in bed early to be ready to work hard again the next day.

typical: average; regular

Building Better Vocabulary

ACTIVITY 20 Word Associations

Circle the word or phrase that is most closely related to the word or phrase on the left. If necessary, use a dictionary to check the meaning of words you do not know.

	A	B
1. successful	negative effect	positive effect
2. an entrepreneur	to be the boss	to have a boss
3. part-time	to work forty hours	to work twenty hours
4. engineering	bridges	orchestras
5. typical	normal	rare
6. a sibling	a brother	an uncle
7. forever	an end	no end
8. servers	an office	a restaurant
9. to separate	to divide	to mix
10. professional	a nice suit	shorts and a t-shirt
11. to wake up	to go to sleep	to stop sleeping
12. traditional	new	old
13. stressful	an earthquake	a picnic
14. athletic	a library	a soccer field
15. requires	must have	optional

ACTIVITY 21   Using Collocations

Fill in each blank with the word that most naturally completes the phrase on the right. If necessary, use a dictionary to check the meaning of words you do not know.

1. make / take   to _____ a friend

2. make / take   to _____ a shower in the morning

3. from / with   to be separated _____ your family

4. at / on   to wake up _____ six in the morning

5. desk / mistake   a common _____

6. in / on   to compete _____ a game

7. in / on   to write _____ the whiteboard

8. of / to   a map _____ the region

9. see / watch   to _____ a television show

10. get / take   to _____ information for a report

ACTIVITY 22   Parts of Speech

Study the word forms. Fill in each blank with the best word form provided. Use the correct form of the verb. If necessary, use a dictionary to check the meaning of words you do not know. (NOTE: The word in bold is the original word that appears in the unit.)

Noun	Verb	Adjective	Sentence Practice
friend / friendship (A PERSON) / (A THING)	Ø	friend**ly**	1. My best _____ lives in Mexico. 2. It is important to be _____ to others.
profess**ion** / profession**al** (A THING) / (A PERSON)	Ø	**professional**	3. Computer graphics is a popular _____. 4. Her _____ experience is impressive.
separa**tion**	**separate**	separate	5. I _____ my clothes before washing them. 6. Jessica and her husband drive _____ cars.
visitor / visit (A PERSON) / (A THING)	**visit**	Ø	7. Wake up! There is a _____ waiting to see you. 8. Every Sunday, Maria _____ her sister.
prefer**ence**	**prefer**	prefer**red**	9. Lisa has a _____ for spicy foods. 10. Ian _____ to go to the beach for his vacations.

Noun endings: *-ship, -ion, -al, -tion, -or, -ence*
Adjective endings: *-ly, -al, -ed*

Original Student Writing

Original Writing Practice

Think about your favorite sport. Then follow these steps for writing about the sport. Put a check (✓) next to each step as you complete it. When you finish your paragraph, use the checklist that follows to edit your work.

_____ STEP 1: In your first sentence, write: _____ *is my favorite sport.* Fill in the blank with the name of the sport.

_____ STEP 2: In your next sentence, write about the first reason you like the sport. Next, write a sentence with an explanation about why you like it.

_____ STEP 3: In the next sentence, write about the second reason that you like the sport. Next, write a sentence with an explanation for this reason.

_____ STEP 4: In the next sentence, write about the final reason that you like the sport. Next, write a sentence with an explanation for this reason.

_____ STEP 5: In the last sentence, give your general opinion about this sport.

_____ STEP 6: Use subject and object pronouns in two of the sentences in STEPS 2 through 4.

_____ STEP 7: Use a possessive adjective in one sentence in STEPS 2 through 4.

_____ STEP 8: Use at least two of the vocabulary words or phrases presented in Activity 20, Activity 21, and Activity 22. Underline these words or phrases in your paragraph.

_____ STEP 9: Go back and look at your sentences. Combine two simple sentences to make one compound sentence.

If you need ideas for words and phrases, see the Useful Vocabulary for Better Writing on pages 147-149.

☑ Checklist

1. ❑ I checked that each sentence has a subject and a verb.

2. ❑ I used the correct tense for all verbs.

3. ❑ I began every sentence with a capital letter.

4. ❑ I capitalized all proper nouns (names, cities, countries, etc.).

5. ❑ I ended every sentence with the correct punctuation.

6. ❑ I used commas correctly in compound sentences.

7. ❑ I gave my paragraph a title.

Exchange papers from Activity 23 with a partner. Read your partner's paragraph. Then use Peer Editing Sheet 2 on ELTNGL.com/sites/els to help you comment on your partner's paragraph. Be sure to offer positive suggestions and comments that will help your partner improve his or her writing. Consider your partner's comments as you revise your own paragraph.

Additional Topics for Writing

Here are ten ideas for journal writing. Choose one or more of them to write about. Follow your teacher's directions. (We recommend that you skip a line after each line that you write. This gives your teacher a place to write comments.)

PHOTO
TOPIC: Look at the photo on pages 62–63. Write about your typical routine for a day of the week. Include the time that you usually wake up, what you eat for breakfast, what your activities are during the day, whom you spend your time with, how you enjoy the day, and what time you go to bed.

TOPIC 2: Choose a member of your family. Write a paragraph about this person. Give general information. Include the person's name, age, nationality, job, hobbies, etc.

TOPIC 3: Write about a special city in a particular country. Include the name of the city, the special tourist attractions, and why it is a special city for you.

TOPIC 4: Write about a job that interests you. Include the title of the job, the duties of the job, and why it is interesting to you.

TOPIC 5: What is your favorite website? Write about a website that you like. What is the address? What kind of information does it have? Why do you like it?

TOPIC 6: Write about your favorite teacher this semester. What is his / her name? What subject does he / she teach? What makes this teacher special?

TOPIC 7: Write about a restaurant that you like. What is the name of this restaurant? Why do you like it? What kind of food does it serve? What is the price range? How is it decorated?

TOPIC 8: Write about your favorite movie. What is the title? Who are the main actors in the movie? What is the story about? Why do you like this movie?

TOPIC 9: Write about a specific food that you know how to cook without using a cookbook. What are the ingredients? Is it easy to prepare? Are the ingredients expensive?

TOPIC 10: Write about a type of music that you do *not* enjoy. Why don't you like it? How does it make you feel when you hear it?

Timed Writing

How quickly can you write in English? There are many times when you must write quickly, such as on a test. It is important to feel comfortable during those times. Timed-writing practice can make you feel better about writing quickly in English.

1. Take out a piece of paper.

2. Read the writing prompt below.

3. Brainstorm ideas for five minutes.

4. Write eight to ten sentences.

5. You have 20 minutes to write.

Describe a typical "free day." What do you normally do during this free time? Who do you like to spend your time with?

Adjectives

**Fishermen on Inle Lake in Myanmar take their
boats out on a beautiful morning.**

OBJECTIVES **Grammar:** To learn about adjectives
Vocabulary and Spelling: To study common words with the sound of <u>o</u> in h<u>o</u>t
Writing: To write about places around the world

*Can you describe
a place you know?*

Grammar for Writing

This **big** bridge is in the United States.

This **long** bridge is in China.

What Is an Adjective?

✓ An **adjective** is a word that describes a noun or a pronoun.

✓ There are different types of adjectives. They all give information about a person, a place, or a thing.

✓ When an adjective and a noun are together, the adjective comes first.

Type of Adjective	Adjectives	Examples in Sentences
Descriptive Adjectives	black, happy, bad, big, hot, difficult, pretty, empty, ready	**Black** clouds mean **bad** weather. Learning English is **difficult**.
Possessive Adjectives	my, your, his, her, its, our, their	**My** car is next to **your** house.
Demonstrative Adjectives	this, that, these, those	**Those** students need **these** pens.
Quantity Adjectives	some, six, ten, many, three	**Many** students have **three** classes.
Nouns Working as Adjectives	all nouns	My **math** exam is difficult. Mr. Miller works in a **pet** store.
Articles*	a, an, the	**A** book is on **the** table.

Descriptive Adjectives

✓ **Descriptive adjectives** describe a noun or a pronoun.

✓ Descriptive adjectives come **before a noun** or **after the verb <u>be</u>** (**am, is, are**).

✓ There is no difference in the form of the adjective for a singular noun or a plural noun.

Singular		Plural	
before a noun:	We have a <u>**new**</u> **clock**.	before a noun:	We have two <u>**new**</u> **clocks**.
after **be**:	Our clock **is** <u>**new**</u>.	after **be**:	Our two clocks **are** <u>**new**</u>.

20 Common Descriptive Adjectives You Need to Know*

1.	another	I have **another** exam tomorrow.
2.	bad	The weather is very **bad** today.
3.	big	They live in a **big** house.
4.	different	Arabic and Korean are **different** languages.
5.	early	I have an **early** class on Monday and Wednesday.
6.	first	My **first** class begins at 8 a.m.
7.	good	This pizza is very **good**.
8.	great	Mona is a **great** friend.
9.	high	People do not like **high** prices.
10.	important	This information is **important** to me.
11.	last	The **last** bus is at 9 p.m.
12.	late	I am always **late** for class.
13.	little	A **little** cat is a kitten.
14.	long	Going from London to Sydney is a **long** trip.
15.	new	Do you have a **new** bed?
16.	next	We are going there **next** Saturday.
17.	old	My grandmother is very **old**.
18.	right	What is the **right** answer to question 5?
19.	same	You and I have the **same** birthday.
20.	young	Michael is a nice **young** man.

Based on the General Service List, Corpus of Contemporary American English, and other corpus sources

Common Endings for Descriptive Adjectives

Many adjectives have a special ending. Three very common endings for adjectives are **–y**, **–ful**, and **–ous**. This list has 32 adjectives with adjective endings. You probably know some of these adjectives already.

Endings	Descriptive Adjectives with –y, –ful, and –ous Endings
–y	angr**y** craz**y** eas**y** funn**y** health**y** hungr**y** rain**y** salt**y** sleep**y** sunn**y** bus**y** dirt**y** empt**y** happ**y** heav**y** laz**y** read**y** scar**y** spic**y** thirst**y**
–ful	beauti**ful** care**ful** color**ful** help**ful** use**ful** wonder**ful**
–ous	danger**ous** delici**ous** fam**ous** jeal**ous** nerv**ous** previ**ous**

Common Student Mistakes

Student Mistake X	Problem	Correct Example ✓
I have a **car red**.	word order	I have a **red car**.
She has ten **reds** apples.	plural adjective	She has ten **red** apples.

ACTIVITY 1 Finding Descriptive Adjectives

These sentences have examples of the 52 descriptive adjectives on page 93. Read the sentences. Then circle the descriptive adjectives in each sentence. The number in parentheses ( ) is the number of descriptive adjectives in that sentence.

1. Your mother is angry about your dirty room. (2)

2. The young girl with a colorful sweater is very sleepy now. (3)

3. Our first names have the same spelling. (2)

4. This spicy pizza is so delicious. (2)

5. Rainy weather makes many people feel sleepy or lazy. (3)

6. High prices for food are very bad for everyone. (2)

7. My old classroom is empty now. (2)

8. The new soccer team from Spain is wonderful. (2)

ACTIVITY 2 Writing Two Sentences with Descriptive Adjectives

Write two sentences with the same descriptive adjective. In the first sentence, put the descriptive adjective before the noun. In the second sentence, use a possessive adjective and the verb **be** (**am, is, are**) to write a new sentence. Be careful with word order.

1. **green**   I have a book.

   before a noun: _____I have a green book._____

   after **be**: _____My book is green._____

2. **good**   They speak English.

   before a noun: _____

   after **be**: _____

3. **fast**   You have a car.

   before a noun: _____

   after **be**: _____

4. good   She speaks Spanish.

before a noun: _____

after **be**: _____

5. big   My father works in an office.

before a noun: _____

after **be**: _____

6. new   My sister has a job.

before a noun: _____

after **be**: _____

7. interesting   My father and my sister have pets.

before a noun: _____

after **be**: _____

8. little   We live in a house.

before a noun: _____

after **be**: _____

Possessive Adjectives

✓ **Possessive adjectives** tell you the owner. These adjectives are:

    my   **your**   **his**   **her**   **its**   **our**   **their**

They come in front of a noun.

✓ There is no difference in the form of the adjective for a singular noun or a plural noun.

    <u>my</u> book, <u>my</u> books

Singular Noun	Plural Noun
subject: **I** have a book. possessive: It is **my** book.	subject: **We** have books. possessive: **Our** books are black.
subject: **You** have a car. possessive: **Your** car is white.	subject: **You** have cars. possessive: Where are **your** cars?
subject: **He** has a watch. possessive: It is **his** watch.	subject: **They** have watches. possessive: **Their** watches are new.
subject: **She** has a bag. possessive: **Her** bag is black.	subject: **They** have bags. possessive: Which are **their** bags?

Common Student Mistakes

Student Mistake X	Problem	Correct Example ✓
Mary has **his** phone.*	wrong possessive adjective	Mary has **her** phone.
They have **theirs** laptops.	plural spelling	They have **their** laptops.
I do not have **me** book.	form of adjective	I do not have **my** book.

*This sentence is possible, but it means Mary has John's phone, not her phone.

ACTIVITY 3 **Using Possessive Adjectives in Connected Sentences**

Complete the sentences with the correct possessive adjectives.

1. John Smith is from the United States. _____ passport is dark blue.

2. Ahmed Al-Turki is from Saudi Arabia. _____ passport is green.

3. Elena Vestri is from Italy. _____ passport is red.

4. My good friend Mei is from China. _____ passport is green.

5. My classmate Gustavo is from Brazil. _____ passport is blue.

6. My sister and I are from Turkey. _____ passports are dark red.

7. Manuel and Gerardo Ramirez are from Mexico. _____ passports are very dark green.

8. Mona is from the United Arab Emirates. _____ passport is dark blue.

9. Kyoko and _____ brother have passports from Japan. _____ passports are red.

10. Enrique and _____ sister have passports from Ecuador. _____ passports are dark red.

ACTIVITY 4 **Using Subjects and Possessive Adjectives in Longer Writing**

Complete the sentences with the correct subjects or possessive adjectives. Be careful with capital letters.

1. Susan likes rings. _____ has many pretty rings. _____ favorite ring is from Turkey.

2. Abdul is from Saudi Arabia. _____ passport is green. _____ speaks Arabic. _____ lives with _____ family in Jeddah.

3. Maria is from Peru. _____ speaks Spanish. _____ works at a big bank. _____ likes _____ job very much. _____ job is not difficult.

4. Maria and Pedro Martinez have two children. _____ children are in high school. _____ are excellent students. _____ son is in 10ᵗʰ grade. _____ name is José. _____ is very hard-working. _____ daughter is in 9ᵗʰ grade. _____ name is Tina. _____ is very smart. _____ is very good at math.

Demonstrative Adjectives

✓ The **demonstrative adjectives** are:
   this, that, these, those
   They come in front of a noun.

✓ **This** and **that** are singular. **These** and **those** are plural.

Meaning	Singular	Plural
near the speaker	<u>This</u> passport is blue.	<u>These</u> passports are blue.
not near the speaker	<u>That</u> passport is red.	<u>Those</u> passports are red.

Common Student Mistakes

Student Mistake X	Problem	Correct Example ✓
<u>These</u> lesson is simple.	plural adjective	**This** lesson is simple.
Are very good these books.	word order	**These books are very good.**

ACTIVITY 5 Using <u>this</u>, <u>that</u>, <u>these</u>, and <u>those</u> in Sentences

Underline the correct demonstrative adjective in each sentence.

1. I can't answer (this, these) exam questions.

2. (That, Those) glass is empty.

3. Who is (this, that) man over there?

4. (This, These) English students are from Colombia.

5. Can you help me with (this, these) question?

6. (This, These) map is the best for your class.

7. The teacher can explain (that, those) grammar lesson again.

8. (That, Those) eggs are for your breakfast tomorrow.

9. Are (that, those) spelling words very difficult?

10. Do you know (that, those) women?

11. (This, These) apple drink is delicious.

12. I really like (this, these) rings a lot.

Nouns Working as Adjectives

✓ **Nouns** can also work as **adjectives** in a sentence. The noun that works as an adjective comes in front of the second noun.

✓ Nouns working as adjectives cannot be plural. Remember that adjectives do not change for singular or plural.

Example of noun (as adjective) + noun	Meaning
my **Tuesday** class	The class is on Tuesday.
a **math** test	The test is about math.
a **tomato** salad	The salad has tomatoes in it.
a **pet** store	The store sells pets.

ACTIVITY 6 Practicing Writing Nouns as Adjectives

Write the first sentence again, but put information from the second sentence in the first sentence. Then write your new sentence. Be careful with word order and adjective form (no plural).

1. Please make a salad. Put tomatoes in the salad.

   Please make a tomato salad.

2. My teacher can answer this question. The question is about math.

   _____

3. These forks are good. The fork is made of plastic.

   _____

4. Please call me on Tuesday. Call me in the afternoon.

   _____

5. I need some shoes. The shoes are for tennis.

   _____

6. I walk to the station every morning. The station is for buses.

   _____

7. This is a book. The book is about rocks.

   _____

8. Let's meet at the shop. The shop sells coffee.

   _____

9. We have an exam tomorrow. The exam is for practice.

   _____

10. Please come to the meeting. The meeting is in the morning.

_____

11. Their garden is big. The garden has vegetables.

_____

12. Their garden is pretty. The garden has flowers.

_____

ACTIVITY 7 **Scrambled Sentences**

Change the order of the words to write a correct sentence. Sometimes more than one answer is possible. Be careful with capitalization, end punctuation, and word order.

1. two yellow cats black on that are taxi

_____

2. tomato salad is this delicious

_____

3. two has big houses our family

_____

4. my three difficult can big sister understand languages

_____

5. like this jim really lemon and his friends drink

_____

6. languages people in many speak two morocco

_____

7. your is difficult last name

_____

8. has three his watch new hands

_____

9. chinese and the red yellow flag is

_____

10. for lettuce those please use fresh salads

_____

ACTIVITY 8 **Finding and Correcting 10 Mistakes**

Circle the ten mistakes. Then write the sentences correctly. The number in parentheses ( ) is the number of mistakes in that sentence. Be ready to explain your answers.

The UAE

1. The UAE mean the United Arab Emirates. (1)

   _____

2. The UAE is a countrys on the persian Gulf. (2)

   _____

3. The UAE has seven emirate. (1)

   _____

4. These emirates Abu Dhabi, Ajman, Dubai, Fujairah, Ras al-Khaimah, Sharjah, and Umm al-Quwain. (1)

   _____

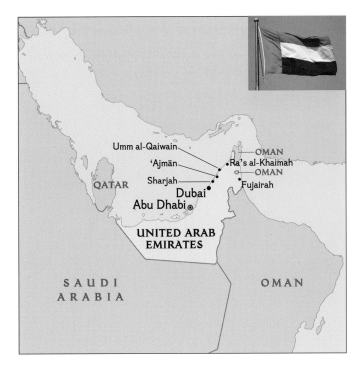

5. The capital are Abu Dhabi. (1)

_____

6. Two countries very near the UAE have Oman and Saudi Arabia. (1)

_____

7. The UAE flag have four color. (2)

_____

8. People from the UAE is Emiratis. (1)

_____

Track 7 •)) ACTIVITY 9 **Dictation**

You will hear six sentences three times. Listen carefully and write the six sentences. The number in parentheses ( ) is the number of words in the sentence. Be careful with capital letters and end punctuation.

1. _____ (5)

2. _____ (6)

3. _____ (7)

4. _____ (5)

5. _____ (9)

6. _____ (8)

Read the sentences in the paragraph very carefully. Fill in the missing words from the word bank. Circle the 27 letters that need to be capital letters. Then copy the paragraph on your own paper.

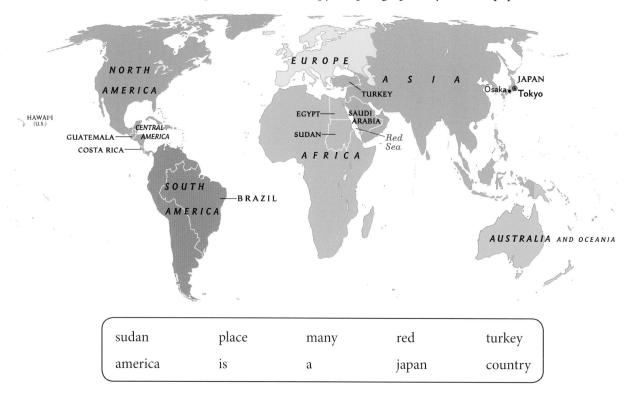

| sudan | place | many | red | turkey |
| america | is | a | japan | country |

Finding Cities and Countries on a World Map

1 here we see a large map with _____ places. 2 tokyo is a large city in

_____ . 3 osaka is _____ large city in japan. 4 costa rica is a country

in central _____ . 5 guatemala is a _____ in central america.

6 the _____ sea is between saudi arabia and egypt. 7 brazil _____

a country in south america. 8 _____ is a country in africa. 9 a part of

_____ is in europe. 10 australia is a very beautiful _____ .

Write the paragraph from Activity 10 again, but make the changes listed below. Sometimes you will have to make other changes, too.

<u>Sentence 1</u>. Change **large** to **colorful**. Add **interesting** to describe **places.**

<u>Sentences 2 and 3</u>. Combine these two sentences. Begin the new sentence with **Tokyo and Osaka …**

<u>Sentences 4 and 5</u>. Combine these two sentences. Begin the new sentence with **Costa Rica and Guatemala …**

<u>Sentences 4 and 5</u>. Add **beautiful** in the correct place.

<u>Sentence 6</u>. Change the order of the countries.

<u>Sentence 7</u>. Add **very big** in the correct place.

<u>Sentence 8</u>. Add **big** in the correct place.

<u>Sentence 9</u>. Add **small** in the correct place.

<u>Sentence 10</u>. Change **very beautiful** to **interesting.**

_____

_____

_____

_____

_____

_____

_____

_____

_____

_____

Building Vocabulary and Spelling

Learning Words with the Sound of o in hot *

o = h **o** t   This sound is usually spelled with the letter **o** and an additional spelling.

h o t

c l o c k

s o c k s

ACTIVITY 12   Which Words Do You Know?

This list has 31 words with the sound of **o** in h**o**t.

1. Notice the spelling patterns.

2. Check ✓ the words you know.

3. Look up new words in a dictionary. Write the meanings in your Vocabulary Notebook.

Common Words

GROUP 1:
Words spelled with **o**

- ☐ **1.** b o d y
- ☐ **2.** b o t h e r
- ☐ **3.** b o t t l e
- ☐ **4.** b o t t o m
- ☐ **5.** b o x
- ☐ **6.** c l o c k
- ☐ **7.** c o m m a
- ☐ **8.** c o m m o n
- ☐ **9.** c o t t o n
- ☐ **10.** d o c t o r
- ☐ **11.** d r o p
- ☐ **12.** e v e r y b o d y

- ☐ **13.** G o d
- ☐ **14.** g o t
- ☐ **15.** h o t
- ☐ **16.** i m p o s s i b l e
- ☐ **17.** j o b
- ☐ **18.** l o c k
- ☐ **19.** l o t
- ☐ **20.** n o t
- ☐ **21.** O c t o b e r
- ☐ **22.** p o s s i b l e
- ☐ **23.** p o t
- ☐ **24.** r o b

- ☐ **25.** r o c k
- ☐ **26.** s h o p
- ☐ **27.** s o c k s
- ☐ **28.** s o m e b o d y
- ☐ **29.** s t o p
- ☐ **30.** t o p

GROUP 2:
Other spelling

- ☐ **31.** f a t h e r

*List is from: Spelling Vocabulary List © 2013 Keith Folse

ACTIVITY 13 Matching Words and Pictures

Use the list in Activity 12 to write the common word that matches the picture.

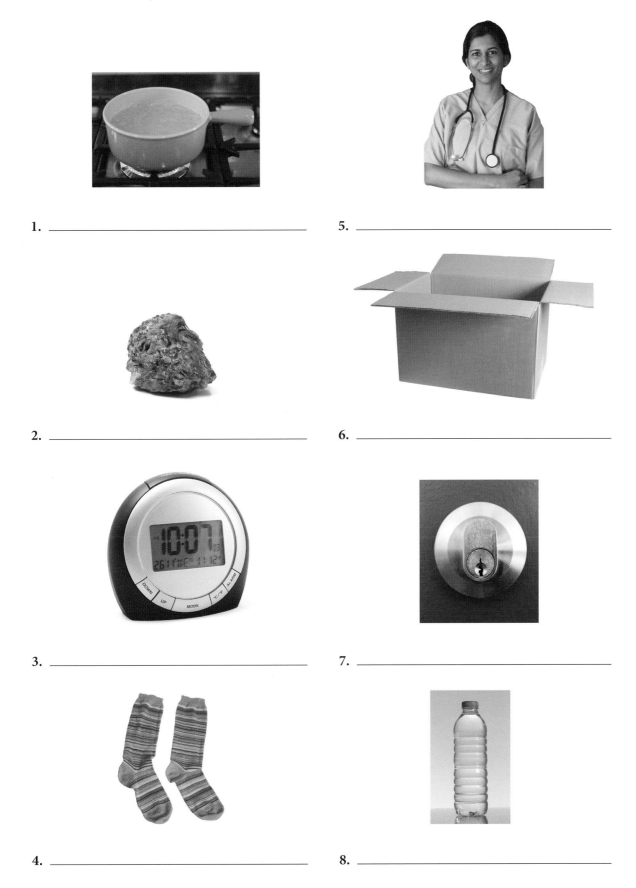

1. _____

2. _____

3. _____

4. _____

5. _____

6. _____

7. _____

8. _____

ACTIVITY 14 Spelling Words with the Sound of o in hot

Fill in the missing letters to spell words with the sound of **o** in h**o**t. Then copy the correct word.

1. j __ b   _____

2. imp __ ssible   _____

3. d __ ctor   _____

4. b __ x   _____

5. g __ t   _____

6. p __ t   _____

7. l __ t   _____

8. c __ mmon   _____

9. h __ t   _____

10. n __ t   _____

ACTIVITY 15 Writing Sentences with Vocabulary in Context

Complete each sentence with the correct word from Activity 14. Then copy the sentence with correct capital letters and end punctuation.

1. the weather in Miami in july is very ....

   _____

2. what is your .... at the company

   _____

3. smith and jones are very .... last names in england

   _____

4. this beautiful .... of chocolates is from your friend

   _____

5. his last name is .... smith

   _____

6. there is a .... of soup on the stove for the children

   _____

7. sick people go to see their ....

   _____

8. yesterday i .... a special letter from the bank

   _____

9. a .... of students in my class have expensive cell phones

   _____

10. a purple cat is ....

   _____

ACTIVITY 16 Scrambled Letters

Change the order of the letters to write a word that has the sound of **o** in h**o**t.

_____	1. o G d	_____	6. b o r
_____	2. y d o b	_____	7. o c k r
_____	3. o p t	_____	8. h e r f a t
_____	4. p h s o	_____	9. o c l k
_____	5. c n m o o m	_____	10. o c l k c

Track 8 ◉⟩) ## ACTIVITY 17 Spelling Practice

Write the word that you hear. You will hear each word two times.

1. _____	6. _____	11. _____
2. _____	7. _____	12. _____
3. _____	8. _____	13. _____
4. _____	9. _____	14. _____
5. _____	10. _____	15. _____

ACTIVITY 18 Spelling Review: Which Word Is Correct?

This review covers the different ways of spelling the sound of **o** in h**o**t in this unit. Read each pair of words. Circle the word that is spelled correctly.

	A	B		A	B
1.	everybady	everybody	11.	drop	drap
2.	fother	father	12.	got	gott
3.	bottle	botle	13.	lot	lat
4.	God	Gad	14.	October	Octaber
5.	imposible	impossible	15.	possible	posible
6.	bodi	body	16.	shap	shop
7.	botom	bottom	17.	soks	socks
8.	bax	box	18.	sombody	somebody
9.	clok	clock	19.	common	comon
10.	coton	cotton	20.	hot	het

Read the four words in each row. Underline the word that is spelled correctly.

	A	B	C	D
1.	bax	box	becks	bocks
2.	limun	limon	lemon	lemun
3.	stop	stap	estop	estap
4.	cammen	cammon	commen	common
5.	frund	frind	frend	friend
6.	rab	rob	rabb	robb
7.	everything	evrithing	everythng	evrithng
8.	sokz	soks	socks	saks
9.	niver	nivor	never	nover
10.	hoppan	hapen	happen	hoppen
11.	drep	drop	drap	drahp
12.	botm	batm	bottom	botom
13.	minit	minute	menit	menute
14.	klok	klock	clok	clock
15.	agin	agen	again	agein
16.	ready	ridy	redy	rady
17.	letle	littl	little	lottle
18.	buzy	busy	bisi	bizi
19.	enstead	insted	instead	ensted
20.	Oktobr	Oktober	October	Octobr

Original Student Writing

Writing Your Ideas in Sentences or a Paragraph

Write five to ten sentences on your own paper. Write about places in the world, such as cities, states, countries, or any places you want. Use adjectives in your sentences. For help, you can follow the examples in Activity 10 (page 102) and Activity 11 (page 103).

Peer Editing

Exchange papers from the above activity. Read your partner's sentences.
Then use Peer Editing Sheet 3 on ELTNGL.com/sites/els to make comments about the writing.

PREPARING TO READ

A Use the words in **blue** to complete the sentences.

> job   city   world   hotel   restaurant

1. We like to eat at that _____ .

2. Alex has a _____ as a teacher in a school.

3. My family stays in a _____ when we travel.

4. London is my favorite _____ .

5. I want to travel all around the _____ .

B Read the questions. Choose the correct answers.

1. Which is a **typical** hair color?
   a. purple   b. brown

2. Which is **large**?
   a. a hospital   b. a cat

3. Which is something that **grows**?
   a. a ball   b. a child

4. Which two words have **different** meanings?
   a. mom / mother   b. mom / dad

C Complete the information to make sentences about you.

1. I am _____ years old.

2. I am a *man / woman*.

3. I *do / do not* live in a city.

4. I work in a/an _____ .

Do you think your answers are "typical" for people around the world?

Holiday travelers pack the Guangzhou Railway Station in Guangdong, China.

THE FACE OF SEVEN BILLION •))) Track 9

There are more than seven billion people in the world. Is there a "most typical" or usual person? Yes, there is. He is a 28-year-old Chinese man. He lives in a city. He can read and write, and he works in a hotel or restaurant.

There are more men than women in the world. China is the country with the largest population. It has over 1.3 billion people. Most people live in cities. Eighty-two percent of the world's population can read and write. Most jobs are in restaurants and hotels.

The faces on page 6 show the typical man and woman today.

What will be the "most typical" person in the future? Every day the world's population grows and changes. Every second, five people are born and two people die. In 1800, there were 1 billion people on Earth. Now, there are more than 7 billion. By 2045, there may be 9 billion. So, the typical person in the future may be very different.

UNDERSTANDING THE READING

UNDERSTANDING
MAIN IDEAS

A Circle the two main ideas of the text.

1. There are more men than women in the world.

2. Is there a "most typical" or usual person? Yes, there is.

3. China is the country with the largest population.

4. The typical person in the future may be very different.

UNDERSTANDING
DETAILS

B Read the questions. Choose the correct answers.

1. How many people are there in China?

   a. over 1.3 billion   b. a million   c. over 5 billion

2. What is the age of the "typical" person?

   a. 18   b. 82   c. 28

3. What percentage of people can read?

   a. fifty   b. eighty-two   c. twenty-eight

4. How many people are born every second?

   a. five   b. one   c. ten

5. How many people are there on earth?

   a. 3 billion   b. 20 billion   c. 7 billion

EXPANDING
UNDERSTANDING

C How are you and the "typical" person the same? How are you and the "typical" person different? Put a check (✓) in the correct column. Then discuss with a partner or write sentences about yourself.

The "typical" person lives in a city. I am the same. I live in a city. I live in Taipei.

The "Typical" Person	Me	
	The Same	Different
1. lives in a city		
2. works in a hotel or restaurant		
3. is 28		
4. is male		
5. lives in China		

PREPARING TO READ

A Read the questions. Choose the correct answers.

1. Which can you **visit**?
   a. New York City   b. soccer

2. What is **popular** on social media?
   a. cat videos   b. telephones

3. Which is a social media **site**?
   a. Windows   b. Facebook

4. Where can you get **news**?
   a. on the Internet   b. in a book

5. Which is another word for *around*?
   a. below   b. about

B Complete the information to make sentences about you.

1. I think the most popular social media site is _____.

2. The social media site I like to visit is _____.

3. I use social media around _____ times a week.

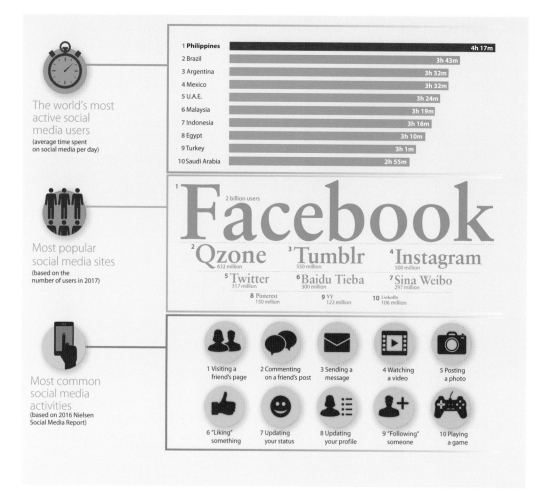

The world's most active social media users
(average time spent on social media per day)

1	Philippines	4h 17m
2	Brazil	3h 43m
3	Argentina	3h 32m
4	Mexico	3h 32m
5	U.A.E.	3h 24m
6	Malaysia	3h 19m
7	Indonesia	3h 16m
8	Egypt	3h 10m
9	Turkey	3h 1m
10	Saudi Arabia	2h 55m

Most popular social media sites
(based on the number of users in 2017)

1 **Facebook** 2 billion users
2 **Qzone** 632 million
3 **Tumblr** 550 million
4 **Instagram** 500 million
5 **Twitter** 317 million
6 **Baidu Tieba** 300 million
7 **Sina Weibo** 297 million
8 Pinterest 150 million
9 YY 122 million
10 LinkedIn 106 million

Most common social media activities
(based on 2016 Nielsen Social Media Report)

1 Visiting a friend's page
2 Commenting on a friend's post
3 Sending a message
4 Watching a video
5 Posting a photo
6 "Liking" something
7 Updating your status
8 Updating your profile
9 "Following" someone
10 Playing a game

A CONNECTED WORLD ·))) Track 10

How much do you use social media?

Social media is a part of many people's everyday lives. Around 2.8 billion people use social media frequently. That's almost 40 percent of the world's population. But how much time do we spend on social media? And how do we use it?

The average person spends two hours and 19 minutes on social media each day. People in the Philippines use it the most. They spend about four hours and 17 minutes on social media every day. Women use social media more than men. In the United States, women spend around two hours more than men on social media each week.

What do people do on social media? Mostly, we look at other people's pages. We visit friends' pages, read their news, and make comments on their posts.

The most popular social media site is Facebook. It has more than 2 billion users. Qzone is a Chinese media site. It is in second place. In 2017, 600 million people around the world used Qzone. That's more than Twitter and Instagram.

Social media continues to grow. There are five new Facebook profiles every second. With more and more people around the world getting Internet access, social media will keep growing.

UNDERSTANDING THE READING

A Circle the two main ideas of the text.

UNDERSTANDING
MAIN IDEAS

1. Social media is very popular.

2. People spend too much time on social media.

3. Social media is growing.

4. Facebook is the most popular social media site.

B Read the questions. Use the text and the infographic on page 114 to choose the correct answers.

INTERPRETING
VISUAL DATA

1. What is the most popular Internet site in the world?

   a. Qzone   b. Facebook   c. Twitter

2. What country uses the most social media each day?

   a. the United States   b. Brazil   c. the Philippines

3. How much time do people in the Philippines spend on social media each day?

   a. 4 hours 17 minutes   b. 3 hours 43 minutes   c. 3 hours 1 minute

4. What is the most common social media activity?

   a. sending a message   b. visiting a friend's page   c. posting a photo

C In what ways do you use social media like most people? In what ways do you use it differently? Put a check (✓) in the correct column. Then discuss with a partner or write sentences about yourself.

EXPANDING
UNDERSTANDING

Most people use social media. I am different. I like to see my friends.

Most People...	Me	
	The Same	Different
1. use social media		
2. spend 2 hours and 19 minutes on social media every day		
3. visit friends' pages		
4. use Facebook		

PREPARING TO READ

BUILDING VOCABULARY

A Use the words in blue to complete the sentences.

> interested in   smart   expensive   earn

1. This shirt is $200. It is _____.

2. I want to learn about airplanes. I'm _____ them.

3. You got an A in science. You are _____.

4. We have jobs. We _____ money.

BUILDING VOCABULARY

B Read the questions. Choose the correct answers.

1. Which is something you can **practice**?
   a. the guitar   b. table

2. Which is something you can **plan**?
   a. a tree   b. a party

3. Which is a **company**?
   a. Microsoft™   b. Monday

4. Which is a **dream**?
   a. eating a sandwich   b. being a scientist

USING VOCABULARY

C Complete the information to make sentences about you.

1. I dream of being a _____.

2. To achieve this dream, first I need to _____.

3. Then I need to _____.

4. I think achieving this dream will be difficult / easy.

Barrington Irving and his plane, *Inspiration*

REACHING FOR THE SKY ⏺ Track 11

In 2007, Barrington Irving became the youngest person to fly alone around the world. He was just 23 years old. He built his own plane. How did he do it?

A PASSION FOR FLYING

Irving became interested in flying at the age of 15. He was in his parents' bookstore in Miami, Florida. There was a customer named Gary Robinson. Robinson was also a pilot. He wanted to teach Irving about flying. Irving didn't think he was smart enough. But Robinson took Irving to an airport. He showed Irving inside a Boeing 777. That changed Irving's life.

Irving really wanted to fly, but flight school was expensive. To achieve his dream, Irving worked different jobs. He washed airplanes. He cleaned swimming pools. At home, he practiced flying with a video game. He earned enough money for school.

CIRCLING THE WORLD

At school, Irving learned to fly. Next, he planned to build a plane. He wanted to fly it around the world alone.

Building the plane was difficult. Irving asked many companies for airplane parts. Three years later, he had the parts. These parts cost $300,000. An airplane company agreed to build a plane with the parts. Soon, Irving's plane was ready.

On March 23, 2007, Irving started his trip. After 97 days, he landed back in Miami. Many people welcomed him home.

SHARING THE DREAM

Irving saw many people in the crowd. This gave him an idea. He wanted to help other young people reach their dreams. Irving says, "Everyone told me what I couldn't do. They said I was too young, that I didn't have enough money. [But] even if no one believes in your dream, you have to pursue[1] it."

[1] When you **pursue** a dream, you try to reach it.

UNDERSTANDING THE READING

A What is the gist of the text?

1. going to school

2. finding an interest

3. achieving a dream

B Put the events in order. Write the number (1–4) next to each.

_____ a. Irving went to flight school.

_____ b. Irving flew around the world

_____ c. Irving got parts for his plane.

_____ d. Irving saw the inside of an airplane.

C Read the information about Barrington Irving. In what ways are you like Irving? In what ways are you different? Put a check (✓) in the correct column. Then discuss with a partner or write sentences about yourself.

Barrington Irving wanted to fly a plane. I don't want to fly a plane. I want to be a doctor.

Barrington Irving	Me	
	The Same	Different
1. had a dream		
2. wanted to fly a plane		
3. believed in following dreams		
4. helped other people achieve dreams		

PREPARING TO READ

A Use the words in **blue** to complete the sentences.

> idea   return   together

1. A: I need to go to the library.
   B: I do too. Let's go _____ .
2. A: Let's go to the park.
   B: That's a great _____ !
3. A: This city is so beautiful.
   B: I hope we can _____ one day.

B Read the questions. Choose the correct answers.

1. Which is a place people **travel** to?
   a. the kitchen   b. Paris

2. Which is **possible**?
   a. flying dogs   b. smiling babies

3. Which is a kind of **show**?
   a. a circus   b. a restaurant

C Complete the information to make sentences about you.

1. A place I once traveled to is _____ .

2. I *do / do not* want to return there.

3. A show I saw is _____ .

4. My _____ and I went to the show together.

Emily Ainsworth (right) with a circus performer in Mexico

A pair of Chilean trapeze artists performs in Circo Atayde, a traveling Mexican circus.

LIFE IN THE RING 🔊 Track 12

Emily Ainsworth loved circuses when she was a child. As she got older, she also became interested in other people and places. "England is a small country," she says. "I saved up for years...so that I could afford to travel abroad."

Ainsworth had many different jobs. At 16, she had enough money to travel to Mexico. Mexico changed her life. She loved the country. She wanted to return one day.

At 22, Ainsworth entered a radio competition[1]. She had to think of an interesting travel idea. If her idea was the best, she could get a free trip. She had an idea for a short movie about Mexican circuses. She wanted to learn about the lives of circus workers there. Ainsworth won the competition and went to Mexico.

Mexico has many circuses. A small one is Circo Padilla. Ainsworth met the circus' ringmaster, Don Humberto. He invited her to visit his circus.

On her first day there, a dancer could not dance in the show. Humberto gave Ainsworth the job. Five minutes later, Ainsworth was in dancer's clothes. She says it was "like a childhood dream come true."

Ainsworth and the other circus workers did shows and lived together. She also studied and took pictures of circus life.

Ainsworth is now a journalist and photographer. She still loves Mexico. She returns there when she can. "I still feel like a part of that world," she says.

Her advice to young people is to follow their childhood dreams. She says, "When you're eight years old, you know that anything is possible."

[1] A competition is when people try to win something.

UNDERSTANDING THE READING

A Circle the main idea of the text.

UNDERSTANDING
MAIN IDEAS

1. Emily Ainsworth loved circuses.

2. Emily Ainsworth followed her childhood dreams.

3. Mexico changed Emily Ainsworth's life.

B Read the questions. Choose the correct answers.

UNDERSTANDING
DETAILS

1. At what age did Ainsworth travel to Mexico?

   a. 16   b. 18   c. 21

2. What circus did Ainsworth work with?

   a. Circo Circo   b. Circo Mexico   c. Circo Padilla

3. What was Ainsworth's job with the circus?

   a. dancer   b. ringmaster   c. photographer

4. What does she say about childhood dreams?

   a. They are funny.   b. They are possible.   c. They are not possible.

C How are you and Ainsworth similar? How are you different? Put a check (✓) in the correct column. Then discuss with a partner or write sentences about yourself.

EXPANDING
UNDERSTANDING

Ainsworth loves the circus. I am the same. I love the circus, too.

Emily Ainsworth	Me	
	The Same	Different
1. loves the circus		
2. is interested in other people and places		
3. had a childhood dream		
4. thinks childhood dreams can come true		

VOCABULARY EXTENSION   UNIT 1

Use superlative adjectives to compare one idea to other ideas. Follow the rules below.

	ADJECTIVE	SUPERLATIVE
- For most short adjectives add -est	fast	the fastest
- For adjectives ending in -e add -st	large	the largest
- For adjectives ending in -y add -iest	busy	the busiest
- For many longer adjectives use *most*	expensive	the most expensive
- For adjectives ending in a vowel and then a consonant, double the final consonant	big	the biggest

A Complete each sentence by writing the correct superlative form of the adjective in parentheses.

1. Beijing is a big city, but _____ (big) city in China is Shanghai.

2. The Duge Bridge is _____ (high) bridge in the world.

3. China had one of _____ (early) human societies in the world.

4. The Shanghai Maglev Train is _____ (fast) train in the world.

5. Soccer is popular in China, but _____ (popular) spectator sport is basketball.

WORD WEB Social Media Words

Below are some common words that appear on social media sites.

Your online **profile** often includes your name, photo, and other personal information.
When you **update** your profile, you change or add new information about yourself.
When you **follow** someone online, you choose to get updates from that person.
A **feed** is the information, stories, or photos you get from people you are following.
If an item on your feed is **trending**, it is very popular right now.

B Match the sentence parts.

1. I added a new photo to my _____   a. trending online.

2. I am interested in music, so I _____   b. profile.

3. I get a lot of news items on my _____   c. follow the most popular bands.

4. Right now, a new cat video is _____   d. feed.

5. I will update my profile because _____ e. I just got married.

VOCABULARY EXTENSION   UNIT 3

Synonyms are words that are very similar in meaning. For example the words *large* and *big* are synonyms.

A Match each word with the correct synonym. Use a dictionary to check your answers.

_____ 1. smart   a. little

_____ 2. begin   b. hard

_____ 3. around   c. start

_____ 4. small   d. about

_____ 5. difficult   e. unhappy

_____ 6. sad   f. clever

B Choose two of the words in exercise **A** and write a sentence using each one.

_____

_____

WORD WEB Time Words and Phrases

We use adverbs of time to describe when an event will happen.
Some adverbs of time do not indicate a specific time.

Soon: in a short time

Later: at some time after now

Someday: an unknown time in the future

Some adverbs of time are more specific.

This weekend

Next year

In five/ten years time

C Complete each sentence with your own ideas.

1. Later today, I plan to _____.

2. This weekend, I plan to _____.

3. Next year, I want to _____.

4. In five years' time, I want to _____.

5. Someday, I hope to _____.

GRAMMAR REFERENCE

UNIT 1
Language for Writing: Simple Present Tense of *Be* and Other Verbs

Be			*Other verbs*	
I	am ('m)	happy. sad. here. at work.	I You We They	**play** soccer. **go** swimming. **have** English class.
You We They	are ('re)			
He She It	is ('s)		He She It	**plays** soccer. **goes** swimming. **has** English class.

EDITING CHECKLIST

Use the checklist to find errors in your writing task for each unit.

	WRITING TASK	
	1	2
1. Is the first word of every sentence capitalized?		
2. Does every sentence end with the correct punctuation?		
3. Does every sentence contain a subject and a verb?		
4. Do your subjects and verbs agree?		
5. Do all possessive nouns have an apostrophe?		
6. Are all proper nouns capitalized?		
7. Is the spelling of places, people, and other proper nouns correct?		

Brief Writer's Handbook

The Parts of a Paragraph

What Is a Paragraph?

A **paragraph** is a group of sentences about **one** specific topic. A paragraph usually has three to ten sentences.

A paragraph is indented. This means there is a white space at the beginning of the first sentence.

Here is a group of sentences that can also be a paragraph.

Sentences	Paragraph
1. I have a big family.	indent ↓ I have a big family. My name is Anna Sanders. I am twenty years old. I study English at my school. I have two brothers. I also have two sisters. I love my brothers and sisters a lot. We are a very happy family.
2. My name is Anna Sanders.	
3. I am twenty years old.	
4. I study English at my school.	
5. I have two brothers.	
6. I also have two sisters.	
7. I love my brothers and sisters a lot.	
8. We are a very happy family.	

Parts of a Paragraph

A paragraph has three main parts: the topic sentence, the body, and a concluding sentence. See the example below that shows these parts.

1. **The Topic Sentence**

   Every good paragraph has a **topic sentence**. The topic sentence tells the main idea of the whole paragraph.

   The topic sentence:

   - is usually the first sentence in the paragraph.

   - should not be too specific or too general.

   If a paragraph does not have a topic sentence, the reader may not know what the paragraph is about. Make sure every paragraph has a topic sentence.

2. The Body

Every good paragraph must have sentences that support the topic sentence. These supporting sentences are called the **body** of a paragraph.

The supporting sentences:

- give more information, such as details or examples, about the topic sentence.

- must be related to the topic sentence.

A good body can make your paragraph stronger. You must be sure to cut out any unrelated or unconnected ideas.

3. The Concluding Sentence

In addition to a topic sentence and body, every good paragraph has a **concluding sentence**. This sentence ends the paragraph with a final thought.

The concluding sentence:

- can give a summary of the information in the paragraph.

- can give information that is similar to the information in the topic sentence.

- can give a suggestion, an opinion, or a prediction.

topic sentence   the body

I have a big family. My name is Anna Sanders. I am twenty years old. I study English at my school. I have two brothers. I also have two sisters. I love my brothers and sisters a lot.

concluding sentence (opinion)

We are a very happy family.

Read each paragraph and answer the questions that follow.

The Best Place to Relax

My back **porch** is my favorite place to **relax**. First, it has lots of comfortable chairs with soft pillows. I feel so good when I sit in them. My back porch is also very peaceful. I can sit and think there. I can even read a great book and nobody **bothers** me. Finally, in the evening, I can sit on my porch and watch the sunset. Watching the beautiful colors always calms me. I can relax in many places, but my back porch is the best.

a porch: a part at the front or back of a house with only a floor and a roof

to relax: to rest or do something enjoyable

to bother: to make someone feel worried or upset

1. How many sentences are in this paragraph? _____

2. What is the main topic of this paragraph? (Circle.)

   a. The writer likes watching the sunset.

   b. The writer likes to read a book in a quiet place.

   c. The writer likes to relax on her back porch.

3. What is the first sentence of this paragraph? (This is the topic sentence.) Write it here.

   _____

   _____

4. The writer gives examples of how her porch is relaxing. List the four things the writer does to relax on her porch.

   a. _The writer sits in comfortable chairs._____

   b. _____

   c. _____

   d. _____

5. Read the paragraph again. Find at least two adjectives and write them below.

   _____

6. Read the topic (first) sentence and the concluding (last) sentence of the paragraph. Write down the ideas that these two sentences have in common.

   _____

Example Paragraph 2

Taipei 101

I work in one of the world's tallest buildings—Taipei 101. This building is in Taipei's business **district**. Taipei 101 opened to the public in 2004. It is made of **steel** and glass panels, so it has a beautiful silver color. It has 101 **floors**. There are even five more levels below the building! Many international businesses have offices in Taipei 101. There are great places to shop in the building, too. I am **proud** to work in such an important place.

a district: an area

steel: a very strong metal

a floor: a level of a building

proud: having a very happy feeling of satisfaction

Post-Reading

1. How many sentences are in this paragraph? _____

2. What is the main topic of this paragraph? (Circle.)

    a. information about a city

    b. information about a person

    c. information about a building

3. What is the first sentence of this paragraph? (This is the topic sentence.) Write it here.

    _____

    _____

4. Answer these questions in complete sentences.

   a. Where is the building?

   _____

   b. How old is the building?

   _____

   c. What color is the building?

   _____

   d. How many floors does the building have in total?

   _____

5. Read the paragraph again. Find at least four adjectives and write them below.

_____

6. Read the topic (first) sentence and the concluding (last) sentence of the paragraph. Write down the ideas that these two sentences have in common.

_____

Parts of a Paragraph: The Topic Sentence

Every good paragraph has a **topic sentence**. The topic sentence is one sentence that tells the main idea of the whole paragraph.

The topic sentence:

- is usually the first sentence in the paragraph
- should not be too specific or too general
- must describe the information in all the sentences of the paragraph

If a paragraph does not have a topic sentence, the reader may be confused because the ideas will not be organized clearly. Make sure every paragraph has a topic sentence!

Practicing Topic Sentences

Read each paragraph and the three topic sentences below it. Choose the best topic sentence and write it on the lines. Then read the paragraph again. Make sure that the topic sentence gives the main idea for the whole paragraph. Remember to indent.

Example Paragraph 3

Beautiful Snow?

_____ Snow is beautiful when it falls. After a few days, the snow is not beautiful anymore. It starts to **melt**, and the clean streets become **messy**. It is difficult to walk anywhere. The **sidewalks** are **slippery**. Snow also causes traffic problems. Some roads are closed. Other roads are **hard** to drive on safely. Drivers have more **accidents** on snowy roads. I understand why some people like snow, but I do not like it very much.

    a. In December, it usually snows.

    b. Some people like snow, but I do not.

    c. I love snow.

to melt: to change from ice to liquid

messy: sloppy; dirty

a sidewalk: a paved walkway on the side of roads

slippery: causing a person to slip or slide, usually because of a smooth surface

hard: difficult

an accident: a car crash

131

Maria and Her Great Job

_____ She works at Papa Joe's Restaurant. She **serves** about 60 people every day. Maria can remember all the dinner orders. If there is a problem with any of the food, she **takes** it **back** to the kitchen **immediately.** Maria works very hard to make sure all her customers have a great meal.

a. My cousin Maria is an excellent server.

b. My cousin Maria works at Papa Joe's Restaurant.

c. Maria's customers do not eat big meals.

to serve: to give someone food and drink at a restaurant

to take back: to return

immediately: at that moment; very quickly

My Favorite City

_____ I love to see all the interesting things there. The city is big, exciting, and full of life. I always visit the Statue of Liberty and the Empire State Building. I also visit Chinatown. At night, I go to **shows** on Broadway. The food in the city is excellent, too. I truly enjoy New York City.

a. I like to see the Statue of Liberty and the Empire State Building.

b. New York is a very big city.

c. My favorite city in the world is New York.

a show: a live performance on stage

Parts of a Paragraph: The Concluding Sentence

In addition to a topic sentence and body, every good paragraph has a **concluding sentence**. The concluding sentence ends the paragraph with a final thought.

The concluding sentence:

- often gives a summary of the information in the paragraph
- often gives information that is similar to the information in the topic sentence
- can be a **suggestion**, **opinion**, or **prediction**
- should <u>not</u> give any new information about the topic

ACTIVITY 3 **Choosing Concluding Sentences**

Read each paragraph and the three concluding sentences below it. Choose the best concluding sentence and write it on the lines. Then read the paragraph again. Make sure that the concluding sentence gives a final thought for the whole paragraph.

Example Paragraph 6

Monday

I hate Monday for many reasons. One reason is work. I get up early to go to work on Monday. After a weekend of fun and relaxation, I do not like to do this. Another reason that I do not like Monday is that I have three meetings every Monday. These meetings last a long time, and they are **extremely** boring. Traffic is also a big problem on Monday. There are more cars on the road on Monday. Drivers are in a bad **mood**, and I must be more careful than usual. _____

_____

extremely: very

a mood: a person's emotion at a particular time

    a. Monday is worse than Tuesday, but it is better than Sunday.

    b. I do not like meetings on Monday.

    c. These are just a few reasons why I do not like Monday.

Buying a Car

Buying a car **requires** careful planning. Do you want a new or a used car? This depends on how much money you can spend. Sometimes a used car needs repairs. What style of car do you want? You can look at many different models to help you decide. Next, do you want extra **features** in your new car? Adding lots of extra features makes a car more expensive. Finally, you have to decide where you will buy your car. _____

_____

to require: to need

a feature: an option, such as a DVD player or tinted windows

   a. It is important to think about all of these things when you are buying a car.

   b. The most important thing is the kind of car that you want to buy.

   c. Will you buy your new car from a friend or a car dealer?

Hanami

Hanami is a very popular Japanese tradition. Every spring, thousands of **cherry** trees bloom all over Japan. For two weeks during Hanami, friends and families gather in parks and the countryside to see the beautiful flowers and celebrate the end of their vacation time. People make lots of food and have huge picnics under the lovely trees. There is lots of music and dancing, and large groups of people walk through the parks together. The celebration often continues into the night, and there are **lanterns** everywhere to light the celebration. _____

a cherry: a small red fruit

a lantern: a light with a decorative cover

a. People like to be with their family and friends during Hanami.

b. Looking at flowers during Hanami is interesting.

c. This is truly a most beloved Japanese custom.

Writing the English Alphabet

A a	B b	C c	D d	E e	F f	G g	H h	I i	J j
K k	L l	M m	N n	O o	P p	Q q	R r	S s	T t
U u	V v	W w	X x	Y y	Z z				

✔ There are 26 letters in the English alphabet.

5 are vowels: A E I O U

21 are consonants: B C D F G H J K L M N P Q R S T V W X Y Z

✔ When **w** and **y** come after a vowel, these two letters are silent vowels: **saw, grow, play, toy, buy.**

✔ When **w** and **y** are at the beginning of a syllable, they are consonant sounds: **wake, wish, when, year, young.**

Definitions of Useful Language Terms

Adjective   An adjective is a word that describes a noun.

Lexi is a very **smart** girl.

Adverb   An adverb is a word that describes a verb, an adjective, or another adverb.

The secretary types **quickly**. She types **very quickly**.

Article   The definite article is *the*. The indefinite articles are *a* and *an*.

The teacher gave **an** assignment to **the** students.
Jillian is eating **a** banana.

Clause   A clause is a group of words that has a subject-verb combination. Sentences can have one or more clauses.

subj.   verb
Roger attends the College of New Jersey.
clause

subj.   verb   subj.   verb
Christopher needs to write his report because **he   wants** to pass the class.
clause 1   clause 2

Noun   A noun is a person, place, thing, or idea.

Sandra likes to eat **sandwiches** for lunch.
Love is a very strong **emotion**.

Object   An object is a word that comes after a transitive verb or a preposition.

Jim bought a new **car**.
I left my **jacket** in the **house**.

Predicate   A predicate is the part of a sentence that shows what a subject does.

subject   predicate
Mr. Johnston walked to the park.

subject   predicate
My neighbor's cat was digging a hole in the yard.

Preposition   A preposition is a word that can show location, time, and direction. Some common prepositions are *around, at, behind, between, from, on, in, near, to, over, under,* and *with*. Prepositions can also consist of two words (*next to*) or three words (*in addition to*).

Punctuation   Punctuation includes the period (.), comma (,), question mark (?), and exclamation point (!).

Subject   The subject of a sentence tells who or what the sentence is about.

My science teacher gave us a homework assignment. **It** was difficult.

Tense   A verb has tense. Tense shows when the action happened.

Simple Present:	She **walks** to school every day.
Present Progressive:	She **is walking** to school now.
Simple Past:	She **walked** to school yesterday.
Past Progressive:	She **was walking** to school when she saw her friend.
Simple Future:	She **is going to walk** to school tomorrow.
Simple Future:	She **will walk** to school tomorrow.

Verb	A verb is a word that shows the action of a sentence.		

They **speak** French.

My father **works** at the power plant.

Review of Verb Tenses

Verb Tense	Affirmative	Negative	Usage
Simple Present	I work you take he studies she does we play they have	I do not work you do not take he does not study she does not do we do not play they do not have	• for routines, habits, and other actions that happen regularly • for facts and general truths
Simple Past	I worked you took he studied she did we played they had	I did not work you did not take he did not study she did not do we did not play they did not have	• for actions that were completed in the past
Present Progressive	I am working you are taking he is studying she is doing we are playing they are having*	I am not working you are not taking he is not studying she is not doing we are not playing they are not having*	• for actions that are happening now • for future actions if a future time adverb is used or understood
Simple Future (*Be Going To*)	I am going to work you are going to take he is going to study she is going to do we are going to play they are going to have	I am not going to work you are not going to take he is not going to study she is not going to do we are not going to play they are not going to have	• for plans that are already made • for predictions based on an action happening in the present
Simple Future (*Will*)	I will work you will take he will study she will do we will play they will have	I will not work you will not take he will not study she will not do we will not play they will not have	• for future plans or decisions that are made at the moment of speaking • for strong predictions • for promises/offers to help
Present Perfect	I have worked you have taken he has studied she has done we have played they have had	I have not worked you have not taken he has not studied she has not done we have not played they have not had	• for actions that began in the past and continue until the present • for actions in the indefinite past time • for repeated actions in the past
Past Progressive	I was working you were taking he was studying she was doing we were playing they were having*	I was not working you were not taking he was not studying she was not doing we were not playing they were not having*	• for longer actions in the past that are interrupted by other actions or events

*Have can be used in progressive tenses only when it has an active meaning in special expressions, such as:

- *have* a party
- *have* a good time
- *have* a bad time
- *have* a baby

Capitalization Rules

1. The first word in a sentence is capitalized.

    I go to the movies every week.

    Deserts are beautiful places to visit.

2. The pronoun *I* is always capitalized.

    Larry and **I** are brothers.

3. People's formal and professional titles begin with capital letters.

    Mr. and **M**rs. Jenkins are on vacation.

    Lisa saw **D**r. Johansen at the bank yesterday.

4. Proper names (specific people and places) begin with capital letters.

    The **C**oliseum in **R**ome is a beautiful old monument.

    Kate met her brother **A**lex at the park.

5. Names of streets begin with capital letters.

    Ruth lives on **W**ilson **A**venue.

6. Geographical locations (cities, states, countries, continents, lakes, and rivers) begin with capital letters.

    I am going to travel to **L**ondon, **E**ngland, next week.

    The **A**rno **R**iver passes through **T**uscany, **I**taly.

7. The names of languages and nationalities begin with capital letters.

    My grandmother speaks **P**olish.

    Jessica is going to learn **J**apanese.

    Melissa is **V**enezuelan, but her husband is **C**uban.

8. Most words in titles of paragraphs, essays, and books are capitalized. The first letter of a title is always capitalized, and the other important words in a title are capitalized. Do not capitalize prepositions (*to, in*), conjunctions (*and, but*), or articles (*a, an, the*) unless they are the first word of the title.

    *The **L**ife of **B**illy **B**arnes*

    Crime and Punishment

    *The **C**atcher in the **R**ye*

    *In the **B**edroom*

9. Specific course names are capitalized.

    Nick is taking **H**istory 101 at 10:00 A.M.

    Nick is taking history this semester. (general subject—no capital letter)

Eight Common Comma Rules

1. Put a comma before *and, but, for, or, nor, so,* and *yet* when they connect two simple sentences. This creates a compound sentence.

    Rick bought Julia a croissant, but he ate it himself.

2. Put a comma between three or more items in a list or series.

    Jen brought a towel, an umbrella, some sunscreen, and a book to the beach.

3. Put a comma after a dependent clause (a clause that begins with a connecting word) when that clause begins a sentence. This is called a complex sentence.

> Because it was raining outside, Alex used his umbrella.

4. Put a comma before or after the name of a person spoken to.

> "Hamad, do you want to play soccer?" Ana asked.

> "Do you want to play soccer, Hamad?" Ana asked.

5. Commas separate parts of dates and places. Put a comma between the day and the date. Put a comma between the date and the year. Put a comma between a city and a state or a country. Put an additional comma after the state or country name if it appears in the middle of a sentence.

> I was born on Tuesday, June 27, 1992.

> The concert was in Busan, Korea.

> The headquarters of that company is located in Osaka, Japan.

> I lived in Phuket, Thailand, for ten years.

6. Use a comma to separate an introductory word or phrase from the rest of the sentence.

> Finally, they decided to ask the police for help.

> Every afternoon after school, I go to the library.

NOTE: *Then* is not followed by a comma.

7. Use a comma to separate information that is not necessary in a sentence.

> Rome, which is the capital of Italy, has a lot of pollution.

> George Washington, the first president of the United States, was a military officer.

8. Put a comma after the salutation in personal letters and after the closing in personal and business letters.

Dear Roberta,	Dear Dr. Gomez,	Dear Ms. Kennedy,
With love,	Sincerely,	Yours truly,
Grandma	Jonathan	Alicia

Spelling Rules for Regular Simple Present Verbs and Plural Nouns

1. Add -*s* to the base form of most verbs and to most nouns.

run	runs
work	works
love	loves

2. If a verb/noun ends in an *x*, *z*, *s*, *sh*, or *ch*, add -*es*.

box	boxes
buzz	buzzes
pass	passes
push	pushes
watch	watches

3. If a verb/noun ends in a consonant + *y*, change the *y* to *i* and add -*es*.

carry	carries
worry	worries
party	parties

4. If a verb/noun ends in a vowel + *y*, add -*s*. Do not change the *y*.

pay	pays
boy	boys
destroy	destroys

5. Add -*es* to *go* and *do*.

go	goes
do	does

Spelling Rules for Regular Simple Past Tense Verbs

1. Add -*ed* to the base form of most verbs.

start	started
finish	finished
wash	washed

2. Add only -*d* when the base form ends in an *e*.

live	lived
care	cared
die	died

3. If a verb ends in a consonant + *y*, change the *y* to *i* and add -*ed*.

dry	dr**i**ed
carry	carr**i**ed
study	stud**i**ed

4. If a verb ends in a vowel + *y*, do not change the *y*. Just add -*ed*.

play	played
stay	stayed
destroy	destroyed

5. If a verb has one syllable and ends in a consonant + vowel + consonant (CVC), double the final consonant and add -*ed*.

stop	sto**pp**ed
CVC	
rob	ro**bb**ed
CVC	

6. If a verb ends in a *w* or *x*, do not double the final consonant. Just add -*ed*.

sew	sewed
mix	mixed

7. If a verb that ends in CVC has two syllables and the <u>second</u> syllable is stressed, double the final consonant and add -*ed*.

ad mit′	admi**tt**ed
oc cur′	occu**rr**ed
per mit′	permi**tt**ed

8. If a verb that ends in CVC has two syllables and the <u>first</u> syllable is stressed, do *not* double the final consonant. Just add -*ed*.

hap′ pen	happe**n**ed
lis′ ten	liste**n**ed
o′ pen	ope**n**ed

Irregular Simple Past Tense Verbs

These are some of the more common irregular verbs in English.

Base Form	Simple Past
be (am/is/are)	was/were
become	became
begin	began
bite	bit
bleed	bled
blow	blew
break	broke
bring	brought
build	built
buy	bought
catch	caught
choose	chose
come	came
cost	cost
cut	cut
do	did
draw	drew
drink	drank
drive	drove
eat	ate
fall	fell
feel	felt
fight	fought
find	found
flee	fled
forget	forgot
get	got
give	gave
grow	grew
have	had
hear	heard
hide	hid
hit	hit
hold	held

Base Form	Simple Past
hurt	hurt
keep	kept
know	knew
leave	left
let	let
lose	lost
make	made
pay	paid
put	put
read	read
run	ran
say	said
see	saw
sell	sold
send	sent
set	set
sing	sang
sink	sank
sit	sat
sleep	slept
speak	spoke
spend	spent
stand	stood
steal	stole
swim	swam
take	took
teach	taught
tell	told
think	thought
throw	threw
understand	understood
wear	wore
win	won
write	wrote

Possessive Pronouns

In general, possessive pronouns are used in spoken English. However, it is important to know how to use them. Possessive pronouns take the place of a possessive adjective + noun combination. In a sentence, a possessive pronoun can be a subject or an object.

Possessive Pronoun	Example
mine	That is not your book. It is **mine** (= my book).
yours (singular)	I don't have my pencil. I need to use **yours** (= your book).
his	My ring is silver, but **his** (= his ring) is gold.
hers	Carol has my cell phone, and I have **hers** (= her cell phone).
ours	Your room is on the first floor. **Ours** (= our room) is on the fifth floor.
yours (plural)	Our class got to have a special party. **Yours** (= your class) did not.
theirs	Jenny likes her class, and Karl and Jim like **theirs** (= their class), too.

Order of Adjectives

Adjectives can go before nouns. When more than one adjective is used before a noun, there is a certain order for the adjectives.

Example: He has a **brown** dog. It is an **enormous** dog.

✗ He has a brown enormous dog.

✓ He has an enormous brown dog.

In general, there are seven kinds of adjectives. They are used in this order:

1. size   *small, large, huge*

2. opinion   *beautiful, nice, ugly*

3. shape   *round, square, oval*

4. condition *broken, damaged, burned*

5. age   *old, young, new*

6. color   *red, white, green*

7. origin   *French, American, Korean*

It is common to have two adjectives before a noun but rare to have three or more adjectives before a noun. When there is more than one adjective before a noun, follow the order above. The noun always goes last. Remember that this list is only a general guideline.

✗ a white Japanese small truck

✓ a small white Japanese truck

✗ a broken large dish

✓ a large broken dish

Quantifiers

Quantifiers give more information about the quantity, or number, of a noun. Quantifiers usually go in front of a noun.

Quantifier	Example
With Count Nouns	
one, two, three (all numbers) a few few many another several a pair of a couple of	**Several** students went to the school office. **Many** people wanted to leave the city. Ellie put **a few** coins in the parking meter.
With Non-count Nouns	
a little little much	There is only a **little** milk left in the refrigerator. We get too **much** homework every night.
With Count or Non-count Nouns	
some (quantity meaning *only*) any a lot of the other other	They got into **a lot of** trouble. Mrs. Jones has **a lot of** friends. Adam does not have **any** money.

The Prepositions *At, On,* and *In*

Prepositions express different ideas. They can indicate time, location, and direction. Remember that a preposition is usually followed by a noun (or pronoun).

Three very common prepositions in English are *at, on,* and *in.* In general, we use *at* with small, specific times and places, *on* with middle-sized times and places, and *in* with larger, more general times and places.

	Time	Place
Small	**at** 1:00 P.M.	**at** the bus stop
Middle	**on** Monday	**on** Bayview Avenue
Large	**in** July **in** spring **in** 2004 **in** this century	**in** Toronto **in** Ontario **in** Canada **in** North America

The Preposition *At*

Location: Use *at* for specific locations.

Angela works **at** the First National Bank.

I always do my homework **at** my desk.

Joel met Jillian **at** the corner of Polk Street and Florida Avenue.

Time: Use *at* for specific times.

My grammar class meets **at** 9:00 A.M. every day.

The lunch meeting begins **at** noon.

Cate does not like to walk alone **at** night.

Direction: Use *at* for motion toward a goal.

My brother threw a ball **at** me.

The robber pointed his gun **at** the policewoman.

The Preposition *On*

Location: Use *on* when there is contact between two objects. We also use *on* with streets.

The picture is **on** the wall.

He put his books **on** the kitchen table.

Erin lives **on** Bayshore Boulevard.

Time: Use *on* with specific days or dates.

Our soccer game is **on** Saturday.

Your dentist appointment is **on** October 14.

I was born **on** June 22, 1988.

The Preposition *In*

Location: Use *in* when something is inside another thing.

The books are **in** the big box.

I left my jacket **in** your car.

Barbara lives **in** Istanbul.

Time: Use *in* for a specific period of time, a specific year, or a future time.

I am going to graduate from college **in** three years.

My best friend got married **in** 2006.

Mr. Johnson always drinks four cups of coffee **in** the morning.

We will meet you **in** ten minutes.

More Prepositions

Here are a few more common prepositions of location. Remember that a preposition is usually followed by a noun (or pronoun). In the chart, the preposition shows the location of the ball (in relation to the box).

Preposition	Example
in	The gift is **in** the box.
on	Marta's gift is **on** the table.
under	Pedro keeps his shoes **under** his bed.
above/over	Sheila held the umbrella **over** her head to stay dry.
between	The milk is **between** the eggs and the butter.
in front of	Mark was standing in **front of** the restaurant.
in back of/behind	My shirt fell **behind** my dresser.
across…from	There is a supermarket **across** the street **from** my house.
next to/beside	The mailman left the package **next to** the door.

Useful Connectors for Writing

Coordinating Conjunctions

Coordinating conjunctions are used to connect two independent clauses (sentences).

Note: A comma usually appears before a coordinating conjunction that separates two independent clauses. (An exception is when the two clauses are both very short.)

Purpose	Coordinating Conjunction	Example
To show reason	for*	He ate a sandwich, **for** he was hungry.
To add information	and	Carla lives in Toronto, **and** she is a student.
To add negative information	nor**	Roberto does not like opera, **nor** does he enjoy hip-hop.
To show contrast	but†	The exam was difficult, **but** everyone passed.
To give a choice	or	We can eat Chinese food, **or** we can order a pizza.
To show concession/contrast	yet†	The exam was difficult, **yet** everyone passed.
To show result	so	It was raining, **so** we decided to stay home last night.

*The conjunction **for** is not common in English. It may be used in literary writing, but it is almost never used in spoken English.

Notice that question word order is used in the clause that follows **nor.

†The conjunctions **but** and **yet** have similar meanings. However, **yet** is generally used to show a stronger contrast.

Many writers remember these conjunctions with the acronym **FANBOYS**. Each letter represents one conjunction: **F** = **for**, **A** = **and**, **N** = **nor**, **B** = **but**, **O** = **or**, **Y** = **yet**, and **S** = **so**.

Subordinating Conjunctions

Subordinating conjunctions are used to connect a dependent clause and an independent clause.

NOTE: When the sentence begins with the dependent clause, a comma should be used after that clause.

Purpose	Subordinating Conjunction	Example
To show reason/cause	because	He ate a sandwich **because** he was hungry.
	since	**Since** he was hungry, he ate a sandwich.
	as	**As** he was hungry, he ate a sandwich.
To show contrast	although	**Although** the exam was difficult, everyone passed.
	even though	**Even though** the exam was difficult, everyone passed.
	though	**Though** the exam was difficult, everyone passed.
	while	Deborah is a dentist **while** John is a doctor.
To show time relationship	after	**After** we ate dinner, we went to a movie.
	before	We ate dinner **before** we went to a movie.
	until	I will not call you **until** I finish studying.
	while	**While** the pasta is cooking, I will cut the vegetables.
	as	**As** I was leaving the office, it started to rain.
To show condition	if	**If** it rains tomorrow, we will stay home.
	even if	We will go to the park **even if** it rains tomorrow.

Useful Vocabulary for Better Writing

Try these useful words and phrases as you write your sentences and paragraphs. They can make your writing sound more academic, natural, and fluent.

Topic Sentences

Words and phrases	Examples
There are QUANTIFIER (ADJECTIVE) SUBJECT…	*There are* many good places to visit in my country.
SUBJECT *must follow* QUANTIFIER (ADJECTIVE) *steps to* VERB…	A tourist *must follow* several simple *steps to* get a visa to visit my country.
There are QUANTIFIER (ADJECTIVE) *types / methods / ways*…	*There are* three different *types* of runners.
It is ADJECTIVE *to* VERB…	*It is* easy *to* make ceviche.

Supporting Sentence Markers

Words and phrases	Examples
One NOUN…	*One* reason to visit my country is the wonderful weather.
Another NOUN… … *another* NOUN	*Another* reason to visit my country is the delicious food. The delicious food is *another* reason to visit my country.
The first / second / next / final NOUN…	*The final* reason to visit my country is its wonderful people.

Giving and Adding Examples

Words and phrases	Examples
For example, S + V. *For instance,* S + V.	My instructor gives us so much homework. *For example*, yesterday he gave us five pages of grammar work.

Concluding Sentences

Words and phrases	Examples
In conclusion, S + V.	*In conclusion,* I believe that my parents are the best in the world.
It is clear that S + V.	*It is clear that* Guatemala is the best tourist destination in South America.
If you follow these important steps in VERB + *-ING*…, S + V.	*If you follow these important steps in* fixing a computer, you will not need to call an expert.

Telling a Story

Words and phrases	Examples
When I was X, *I would* VERB…	*When I was* a teenager, *I would* go to the beach with my friends every day.
When I think about that time, S + V.	*When I think about that time*, I remember my grandparents' love for me.
I will never forget NOUN…	*I will never forget* the day I left my country.
I can still remember NOUN… *I will always remember* NOUN…	*I can still remember* the day I started my first job.
X *was the best / worst day of my life.*	My sixteenth birthday *was the best day of my life.*
Every time S +V, S + V.	*Every time* I tried to speak English, my tongue refused to work!

Describing a Process

Words and phrases	Examples
First (*Second, Third*, etc.), *Next*, … / *After that*, … / *Then* … *Finally*, …	*First*, you cut the fish and vegetables into small pieces. *Next*, you add the lime juice. *After that*, you add in the seasonings. *Finally*, you mix everything together well.
The first thing you should do is VERB…	*The first thing you should do is* wash your hands.
Before S + V, S + V.	*Before* you cut up the vegetables, you need to wash them.
After / When S + V, S + V. *After that*, S + V.	*After* you cut up the vegetables, you need to add them to the salad. *After that*, you need to mix the ingredients.
The last / final step is… *Finally*, …	*The last step is* adding your favorite salad dressing. *Finally*, you should add your favorite salad dressing.

Showing Cause and Effect

Words and phrases	Examples
Because S+ V, S + V. S + V *because* S + V. *Because of* NOUN, S + V. S + V *because of* NOUN.	*Because* I broke my leg, I could not move. I could not move *because* I broke my leg. *Because of* my broken leg, I could not move. I could not move *because of* my broken leg.
CAUSE, *so* RESULT.	My sister did not know what to do, *so* she asked my mother for advice.

Describing

Words and phrases	Examples
Prepositions of location: *above, across, around, in, near, under*…	The children raced their bikes *around* the school.
Descriptive adjectives: *wonderful, delightful, dangerous, informative, rusty*…	The *bent, rusty* bike squeaked when I rode it.
SUBJECT + *BE* + ADJECTIVE.	The Terra Cotta Warriors of Xian *are amazing*.
SUBJECT + *BE* + *the most* ADJECTIVE + NOUN.	To me, Thailand *is the most* interesting country in the world.
SUBJECT *tastes / looks / smells / feels like* NOUN.	My ID card *looks like* a credit card.

SUBJECT + *BE* + *known / famous for its* NOUN.	France *is famous for its* cheese.
Adverbs of manner: *quickly, slowly, quietly, happily…*	I *quickly* wrote his phone number on a scrap of paper that I found on the table.

Stating an Opinion

Words and phrases	Examples
Personally, I believe / think / feel / agree / disagree / suppose (*that*) S + V.	*Personally, I believe that* New York City should ban large sugary drinks.
VERB + *-ING should not be allowed.*	*Smoking* in public *should not be allowed.*
In my opinion / view / experience, S + V.	*In my opinion,* smoking is rude.
For this reason, S + V. *That is why I think that* S + V.	*That is why I think that* smoking should not be allowed in restaurants.
There are many benefits / advantages to VERB + *-ING.*	*There are many benefits to* swimming every day.
There are many drawbacks / disadvantages to VERB + *-ING.*	*There are many drawbacks to* eating most of your meals at a restaurant.
I prefer X [NOUN] *to* Y [NOUN].	*I prefer* soccer *to* football.
To me, VERB + *-ING makes* (*perfect*) *sense.*	*To me,* exercising every day *makes perfect sense.*
For all of these important reasons, I think / believe (*that*) S + V.	*For all of these important reasons, I think* smoking is bad for your health.

Arguing and Persuading

Words and phrases	Examples
It is important to remember that S+V.	*It is important to remember that* students only wear their uniforms during school hours.
According to a recent survey / poll, S + V.	*According to a recent poll,* 85 percent of high school students felt they had too much homework.
Even more important, S + V.	*Even more important,* statistics show the positive effects of school uniforms on student behavior.
SUBJECT *must / should / ought to* VERB.	Researchers *must* stop unethical animal testing.
I agree that S + V. *However,* S + V.	*I agree that* eating healthily is important. *However,* the government should not make food choices for us.

Reacting/Responding

Words and phrases	Examples
TITLE *by* AUTHOR *is a / an* (ADJECTIVE) NOUN.	*Harry Potter and the Goblet of Fire* by J.K. Rowling *is an* entertaining book to read.
My first reaction to the prompt / news / article / question was / is NOUN.	*My first reaction to the article was* anger.
When I read / looked at / thought about NOUN, *I was amazed / shocked / surprised…*	*When I read* the article, *I was surprised* to learn of his athletic ability.

Building Better Sentences

Being a good writer involves many skills including correct grammar usage, varied vocabulary, and conciseness (avoiding unnecessary words). Some student writers like to keep their sentences simple. They feel that they will make mistakes if they write longer, more complicated sentences. However, writing short, choppy sentences one after the other is not considered appropriate in academic writing. Study the examples below.

The time was yesterday.

It was afternoon.

There was a storm.

The storm was strong.

The movement of the storm was quick.

The storm moved towards the coast.

The coast was in North Carolina.

Notice that every sentence has an important piece of information. A good writer would not write all these sentences separately. Instead, the most important information from each sentence can be used to create ONE longer, coherent sentence.

Read the sentences again; this time, the important information has been circled.

The time was (yesterday.)

It was (afternoon.)

There was a (storm.)

The storm was (strong.)

The (movement) of the storm was (quick.)

The storm (moved towards the coast.)

The coast was in (North Carolina.)

Here are some strategies for taking the circled information and creating a new sentence.

1. Create time phrases to begin or end a sentence: yesterday + afternoon

2. Find the key noun: storm

3. Find key adjectives: strong

4. Create noun phrases: a strong + storm

5. Change word forms: movement = move; quick = quickly
   moved + quickly

6. Create place phrases: towards the coast

   towards the coast (of North Carolina)

   or

   towards the North Carolina coast

Better Sentence:

Yesterday afternoon, a strong storm moved quickly towards the North Carolina coast.

Here are some other strategies for building better sentences.

7. Use connectors and transition words.

8. Use pronouns to replace frequently used nouns.

9. Use possessive adjectives and pronouns.

   Study the following example:

   (Susan) (went) somewhere. That place was (the mall.) Susan wanted to (buy new shoes.)
   The shoes were for (Susan's mother.)

Improved, Longer Sentence:

   Susan went to the mall because she wanted to buy new shoes for her mother.

Practices

   Follow these steps for each practice:

Step 1: Read the sentences. Circle the most important information in each sentence.

Step 2: Write an original sentence from the information you circled. Remember that there is more than
one way to combine sentences.

Practice 1

A. 1. (Tina) is my (friend.)

   2. Tina (works.)

   3. The work is at (Washington Central Bank.)

   <u>My friend Tina works at Washington Central Bank.</u>

   _____

B. 1. There are boxes.

   2. The boxes are on the table.

   3. The boxes are heavy.

   _____

   _____

C. 1. Caroline attends classes.

   2. The classes are at Jefferson Community College.

   3. The classes are on Wednesdays.

   _____

   _____

D. 1. Tuscany is a region.

   2. This region is in Italy.

   3. This region is beautiful.

   _____

   _____

Practice 2

A. 1. There are books.

   2. The books are rare.

   3. The books are in the library.

_____

_____

B. 1. Drivers have more accidents.

   2. The accidents happen on roads.

   3. The roads are snowy.

_____

_____

C. 1. Aspirin is good for headaches.

   2. Aspirin is good for colds.

   3. Aspirin is good for pain.

_____

_____

Practice 3

A. 1. Charlie is a man.

   2. Charlie is my uncle.

   3. Charlie works hard in a restaurant.

   4. The restaurant belongs to Charlie.

_____

_____

B. 1. Tourists often ride boats.

   2. The boats are on the Seine River.

   3. Tourists do this at night.

   4. Tourists do this to see the Eiffel Tower's lights.

   5. The tower's lights are beautiful.

_____

_____

C. 1. Steven is in bed.

    2. It is early.

    3. Steven does this to be ready to work hard.

    4. He is doing this again.

    5. His work is the next day.

_____

_____

Practice 4

A. (Hint: Use a coordinating conjunction.)

    1. Chavez's family received money.

    2. There was very little money.

    3. People treated them badly.

_____

_____

B. (Hint: Use a coordinating conjunction.)

    1. My parents were not rich.

    2. My parents were always happy.

_____

_____

C. 1. This book gives us information.

    2. There is a lot of information.

    3. The book gives us the information now.

    4. The information is important.

    5. The information is about life in the fourteenth century.

_____

_____

Practice 5

A. (Hint: Use a coordinating conjunction.)

    1. Angela needs to buy some fruits.

    2. Angela needs to buy some vegetables.

    3. Angela is shopping at the farmer's market.

_____

_____

B. 1. Visitors are standing in line.

    2. There are many visitors.

    3. The visitors are also waiting to take pictures.

    4. The pictures are of themselves.

    5. There are ruins in the background.

_____

_____

C. (Hint: Use a coordinating conjunction.)

    1. Lisana is working.

    2. This company works with computers.

    3. Lisana does not have a computer engineering degree.

_____

_____

Practice 6

A. (HINT: Create a complex sentence.)

    1. First, Carmen arrives.

    2. Then Carmen will perform some dances.

    3. These dances will be formal.

    4. Carmen will do these dances with her friends.

_____

_____

B. (HINT: Create a complex sentence.)

    1. I go to the theater.

    2. The theater is on Broadway.

    3. I do this often.

    4. The reason I do this is that I live in New York.

_____

_____

C. (HINT: Create a complex sentence.)

1. First, I will arrive in Canada.

2. Next, I am going to buy a lot of souvenirs.

3. There will be souvenirs for my parents.

4. There will be souvenirs for my brother.

5. There will be souvenirs for my friends.

_____

_____

Practice 7

A. (HINT: Use an adjective clause.)

1. The two women are my grandmother and my mother.

2. The women are sitting on the sofa.

_____

_____

B. (HINT: Use an adjective clause.)

1. These are words.

2. There are just a few of these words.

3. These words cause problems for English speakers.

4. These problems are with spelling.

5. These speakers are native and nonnative.

_____

_____

C. 1. Jenna is eating lunch.

2. Jenna is talking to her friends.

3. Jenna is in the cafeteria.

4. Jenna is doing these things right now.

_____

_____

NOTES

NOTES

NOTES

NOTES

NOTES

NOTES

NOTES